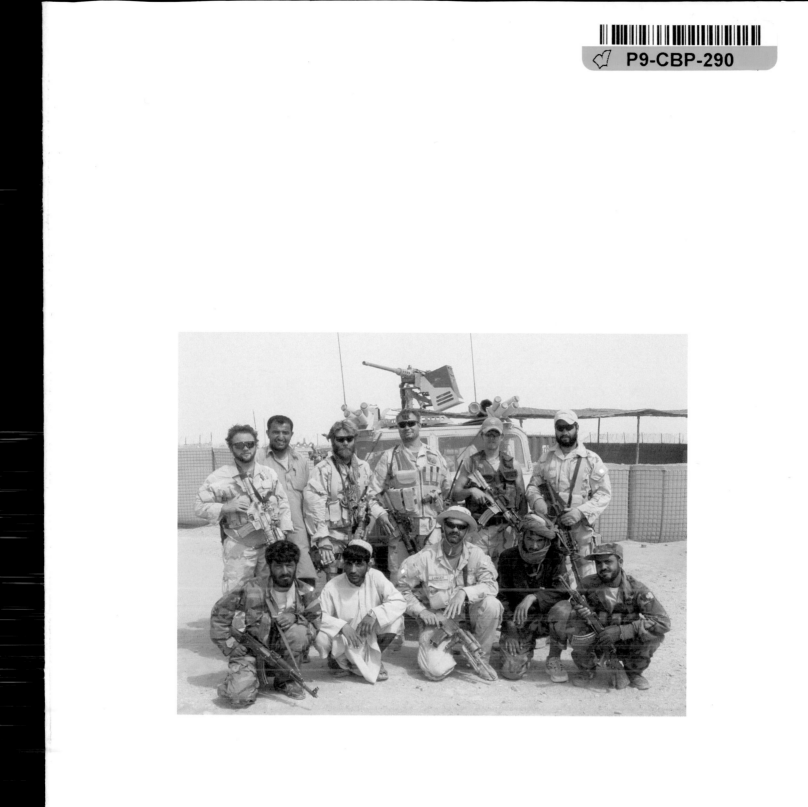

TO BE A U.S. ARMY GREEN BERET

COLONEL GERALD SCHUMACHER
UNITED STATES ARMY SPECIAL FORCES (RET.)

ZENITH
PRESS

To my son Kevin Patrick Schumacher,
who has been my point man
since the day he stepped into my life.

First published in 2005 by Zenith Press, an imprint of MBI
Publishing Company, Galtier Plaza, Suite 200, 380 Jackson Street,
St. Paul, MN 55101-3885 USA

Zenith Press titles are also available at discounts in bulk quantity
for industrial or sales-promotional use. For details write to
Special Sales Manager at MBI Publishing Company, Galtier Plaza,
Suite 200, 380 Jackson Street, St. Paul, MN 55101-3885 USA.

ISBN 0-7603-2107-8

Edited by Steve Gansen
Designed by Russ Kuepper

Printed in China

On the cover: Special Forces soldiers (a.k.a. Green Berets) come
from all walks of life and all branches of the service. The soldier
on the cover is Master Sergeant Rick Cardin. He was initially an
Army combat engineer for four years and then spent two years in
military intelligence. He then left active duty and worked for
several years in law enforcement for a California county sheriff's
department. He later rejoined the Army, was accepted in the
Special Forces training program, and subsequently served in
several different Special Forces Groups. Rick Cardin now owns
and operates a private security firm specializing in asset
protection and executive security. Many U.S. firms conducting
international business in high risk areas seek out the services of
men who are former Green Berets.

On the frontispiece: A Special Forces Operational Detachment
Alpha (ODA) from the 3rd Special Forces Group in Afghanistan
pose for a photo with their Northern Alliance resistance fighters
before departing on a combat patrol.

On the title page: Although SCUBA is a primary area of
concentration for Navy SEALs, SF teams frequently infiltrate by
water. This student has just completed an underwater navigation
training exercise at the Army's Combat Diver Qualification
Course in Key West, Florida. The student is wearing the LAR V
Dragger rebreather, which eliminates telltale bubbles rising to the
surface. © *Hans Halberstadt*

On the table of contents: A Special Forces soldier moves through
the jungle with an FN-MAG 58 machine gun. The MAG 58 is a
close cousin to the U.S. military's 7.62mm M60 and is used by
more than eighty countries. The weapon incorporates features
from Browning's tried and true M1918 BAR. The action has been
turned upside-down and modified to accept belt feed. Green
Berets must become as familiar with foreign weapons as they are
with U.S.-made firearms.

On the back cover, left: Special Forces soldiers are often in some
of the most dangerous combat situations. It is not uncommon for
them to have earned medals for heroism, but their heroic actions
often go unnoticed as they operate independently and behind
enemy lines. On this occasion their actions were noticed.
Lieutenant General Philip R. Kensinger Jr. awards decorations for
valor during combat operations to members of the "Desert
Eagles" (1st Battalion, 3rd Special Forces Group). The 3rd Special
Forces Group infiltrated early into Afghanistan, and as that war
wound down they deployed directly into combat in Iraq. Both of
these SF soldiers have just received the Silver Star. The NCO in
the foreground is also receiving a Purple Heart. **Top right:** A
resistance fighter, armed with an AK47 and 30-round "banana
clip" magazine, is in position for the final assault. If the student
ODA fails to plan and advise properly for critical events of the
operation, the Gs will make certain that the unplanned segment
goes haywire. The ODA will be faced with unexpected problems
and challenges as a consequence of poor prior planning. A good
plan has "what-if'd" every course of action and every
contingency. SF soldiers must be experts in analyzing plans.
© *Hans Halberstadt.* **Bottom right:** Although Special Forces
soldiers normally maintain a low profile, this pair of smiling
Green Berets have attached the American flag to the radio
antenna of their heavily armed Humvee in a rare open display of
patriotic fervor as they return from a combat operation.

Author bio:
A captain in Vietnam in the 1960s, Gerry Schumacher went on to
command a variety of post-Vietnam missions before his 1997
retirement at the rank of colonel. One of the projects under his
command in the late 1980s was the use of Special Forces units to
test the security of defense installations such as ballistic missile
early warning sites (BMEWs), radio relay sites, radar posts,
ammunition storage facilities, and power plants.

Schumacher retired as a colonel in 1997, after 32 years of
service with the U.S. Army and U.S. Army Reserves. He spent over
20 of those years in Special Forces. He has been a guest lecturer at
preeminent "think-tank" groups and has appeared many times on
network television and national radio. He is a graduate of the
University of Miami and numerous military academic
institutions. He resides in Marin County, California.

CONTENTS

Acknowledgments

One of the most important objectives in the development of this book was to compare Special Forces training to actual Special Forces Operations. To that end, I am deeply indebted to Sergeant First Class Kenneth Stearns for the time, effort, and unique insights he provided. SFC Stearns has served with the 5th, 7th, and 19th Special Forces Group. He has also been a survival, escape, evasion, and resistance (SERE) instructor in the 1st Special Warfare Training Group at Fort Bragg, aka, "the schoolhouse." In spite of his hectic schedule, he accommodated many interviews, visits, and dozens of phone calls from me. SFC Stearns was instrumental in making this book come to life.

Many thanks to Captain Karl Johnson, a 19th Special Forces Group detachment commander who provided thoughtful insights comparing his Q-course experiences to his recently completed missions in the Persian Gulf area. Also, my heartfelt appreciation goes to Sergeant "O" for his input and review of the Special Forces Assessment and Selection chapter. And to the many SF NCOs and officers that requested, for both personal and security reasons, to remain anonymous, thank you. Your stories were revealing, humorous, candid, and colorful. I used many of them throughout the book. A special acknowledgment is tendered to the anonymous team medical NCO who related the story of the conundrum of SF medics. Thanks again.

A big nod of appreciation to the Department of the Army, Public Affairs Director, New York office, Mr. Bruce Zielsdorf, for the original book concept approval. Thanks to Sergeant Major Morgan, 1st Special Warfare Training Group, for his input on course content and the process of becoming SF qualified. Thank you to Fred Pushies for providing so many tremendous photographs for this endeavor. Kudos to Kelly Worden, the radio talk show host and martial arts instructor who trains with Special Forces and supports them on his show to tens of

thousands of listeners across the country. A very special thank you goes to my longtime friend, Ben Parsons, who kindly and thoughtfully reviewed each chapter and provided his visceral reaction to the book as he tolerated my constant interruptions of his daily life.

I'd like to offer a special thanks to several men that had a major influence on my career in Special Forces, and they are reflected in some of the vignettes in this book. In particular I wish to offer my deepest appreciation to my mentor, Major General William Cockerham, for trusting in me over and over again and teaching me more than a thing or two about the military decision-making process. Thank you to my good friend, Colonel Stephen Leopold, who, despite suffering horrific experiences during his many years as a POW, returned to Southeast Asia, on his own, to personally search for missing comrades. Steve, you epitomize the most courageous elements of the army's standing order to never leave a fallen comrade on the battlefield. It is with deepest respect and gratitude that I thank Lieutenant Colonel Mickey Krier, who exuded all the finest qualities of the quiet professional. Mickey consistently set the example of a no-nonsense, stay alive, get the job done, and keep it to yourself soldier.

Much appreciation is offered to Chief Warrant Officer James Gaston, and Command Sergeant Major Russ Mann, who exemplify the most professional attributes found in the Special Forces Warrant and the Non-Commissioned Officer ranks. Every commander that has ever had the privilege and honor of serving with either of you has been made to look better because of you. We all owe you much.

It is unlikely that I would have pursued a Special Forces career had I not, by chance, shared the same compound with the Special Forces team No. A-502, at Dien Khanh District, Khanh Hoa Province in the Republic of Vietnam. As a Mobile Advisory Team leader and later as the District Senior Advisor, I shared responsibility with the Special Forces team for the security of the compound and security of the District's strategic areas. I was able to witness, firsthand, that the SF team members knew their trade and were far better trained for unconventional warfare missions than were regular army units. It was only a matter of time before I joined Special Forces. My sincere thanks to what was, with over 50 SF soldiers guiding twelve Montangard companies, the largest "A" team in the army.

I have reserved a very special thanks and debt of gratitude, to my good friend of 20 years, Hans Halberstadt. Hans has written countless books on Special Operations Forces and provided so many of the photographs in this book. Since the day Hans recommended me to author this project, he has politely put up with dozens of phone calls, meetings, and E-mails from me as I began putting pen to paper. Thank you, Hans, I am deeply indebted to you. You went far beyond the call of duty.

And finally, to my wife, who tolerated many months of my obsession with this book, listened patiently to every word that she had already heard or read a dozen times before, and always kept my ego in check: thanks, Deb.

A Special Forces Operational Detachment Alpha (ODA) from the 3rd Special Forces Group pauses for a moment for this photo prior to launching combat operations deep in the mountains of Afghanistan. These men have "been there and done that." This book is about how they became U.S. Army Green Berets.

ONE

Special Forces combat divers from the 7th Special Forces Group at Fort Bragg, North Carolina, fast rope from an MH-60 Black Hawk helicopter onto the deck of a Navy submarine at sea. This type of linkup can be used in both infiltration and extraction operations. Although Special Operations amphibious missions are the primary responsibility of Navy SEALs, Army Special Forces also trains teams to execute waterborne operations.

Twelve Traits of a Green Beret

It has been said that life is a journey, not a destination. Becoming a Green Beret is an endless process of developing skills, testing them, employing them, and developing new skills. A U.S. Army Green Beret, officially referred to as Special Forces, is never finished with training. For a Special Forces (SF) soldier, graduation from the six-phase qualification program and receipt of a Special Forces tab is not the culmination of training. Many professions participate in extensive, ongoing career-development programs after initial graduation, but, as you will see, Special Forces is clearly unique in the magnitude and scope of ongoing training requirements. Attaining the Special Forces tab is just the beginning. It is a "license to practice."

If you seek attention, look for public recognition, think you'd like to tell people that you are a Green Beret, enjoy showing your skills, are excited about the prospect of discussing your travels, or if you'd like to tell the world what it is you have experienced, then you need to explore a different branch of the military. Special Forces *is not* for you.

As a Green Beret, you will go to far-off places, live with the local people, see new things, experience interesting cultures, survive behind enemy lines, train foreign soldiers, hunt down terrorists, set explosives, deliver babies, jump out of airplanes, rappel from helicopters, heal the wounded, help establish local governments, train police forces, dig wells and farm fields, and build bridges.

When you come home, you'll go through another training program. It could be learning another foreign language, underwater operations, military free fall, or cold-weather survival. Shortly after that, you'll be gone again, on a different mission in a different country with a different enemy and a different challenge. Your new mission could be in the Arctic, the desert, the jungle, mountains, a city, or at sea. Maybe you'll ride horses into battle this time. It just depends on the best way to get the job done. That's why you are a Green Beret. How do you explain that to anyone? You don't!

In the making of a Special Forces soldier, the Army gains a truly intelligent, creative, resourceful, and humanitarian resource. This new breed of warrior goes far beyond the historic definition of "soldier." Special Forces soldiers employ levels of vision, compassion, ingenuity, technology, medical skills, construction assets, cunning, ruthlessness, and stamina not found in traditional soldiers. The initial qualification training to become a Green Beret is unquestionably longer, more academically focused, and collectively more physically demanding than any of the other special operations training programs.

An Army Special Forces soldier in Afghanistan with his Northern Alliance tribal fighters. These are the types of people and this is the environment in which Green Berets must learn to fight and survive. Facial hair is customary among mature men in the tribe. To be accepted, Green Berets will often go "native." It is not uncommon for SF soldiers to become close friends with the indigenous fighters. Many Kurdish tribesmen have named their children, "Bob, Jake, Chief, or Top," after an SF soldier who fought side by side with them. The "0 Pos" lettering on his sleeve is his blood type in the event he is wounded in action and requires a blood transfusion.

1st SPECIAL FORCES GROUP (AIRBORNE)

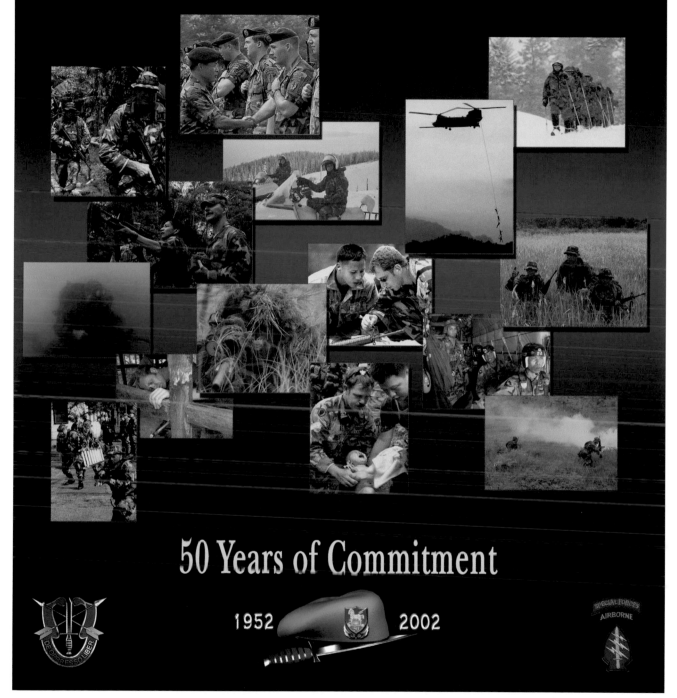

50 Years of Commitment

1952　2002

Many are called, but few are chosen. This Special Forces recruiting poster from the 1st Special Forces Group soliciting volunteers for SF training suggests that you, too, could be a Green Beret, and maybe you can. The percentage of men who complete Special Forces training is so small that the Special Forces Command is probably on par with the best of the New York ad agencies in encouraging soldiers into the training pipeline.

Since SF frequently operates deep in enemy territory and without immediate reinforcements available, they go in "armed to the teeth." This 19th Special Forces Group soldier mans his M60 machine gun while the roof is lined with antitank weapons that are useful in a variety of combat situations.

Green Berets have a broader spectrum of missions than the other Special Operation Forces (SOFs). SOF refers to all units whose basic charter is to conduct special operations missions, including Rangers, Navy SEALS, Army Civil Affairs, Psychological Operations Units, Army Special Operations Aviation, Air Force Special Operations Wing, and Pararescue. The title "Special Forces" relates exclusively to the U.S. Army Special Forces, often referred to as Green Berets. SF training prepares soldiers for living with foreign fighters over long periods of time, often behind enemy lines. They are capable of being completely self-sufficient and conducting independent operations without contact or logistical support from the outside. They share with other SOF organizations the ability to conduct direct-action and special reconnaissance missions, but that is where the commonality stops. Green Beret expertise in

Unconventional Warfare is unsurpassed. SF teams are equally adept at providing training to soldiers in both developed countries and Third World nations. Green Berets are often referred to as "force multipliers." History is replete with stories of U.S. Army SF detachments successfully recruiting, training, and guiding thousands of otherwise defeated people into winning battles against tyrannical enemies. They are *De Oppresso Liber*, Liberators of the Oppressed.

Recently, some military strategists suggested that wars could be won with technology alone. We have now learned that much of that technology only works against a conventional enemy. Special Forces is the technology that is best equipped to combat the types of "non-nation-state" enemies (terrorists) that we now find ourselves facing. The need for Special Forces soldiers has never been greater.

To Be a U.S. Army Green Beret is not merely a step-by-step analysis of a physical and educational process men must pass through en route to becoming qualified for Special Forces. It is a glimpse into the soul and character of the men who seek out this career path, complete this training, master these skills, and execute the missions unique to the Army's Special Forces.

Special Forces teams frequently conduct operations that have strategic implications for our national security. The manner in which they conduct themselves and the success or failure of an SF mission can have a powerful and lasting impact on the relations of the United States with other nations. For this reason, a Special Forces candidate must exhibit a level of maturity well beyond his years. For many years, Special Forces would not even consider accepting an officer or enlisted man into its training program with fewer than three years of previous military experience. Given the current worldwide demands on Special Forces units, the Army is making exceptions for exceptional applicants.

What kind of person makes it as a Green Beret? What kind of men can make something out of nothing and stay with the mission when every fiber in their body says quit? What kind of men will think about how the enemy thinks, eats, feels, and sleeps? What type of soldier will spend as much time taking care of sick villagers as he will tracking the enemy? What does it take to develop men who will propose solutions that kill and destroy nothing, yet win the peace? Where do these men come from? What are the distinguishing characteristics of Green Berets?

The base requirements for consideration to enlist in the Special Forces training program are: You must be a male between 18 and 30 years of age (SF is not open to women). You must be a U.S. citizen and a high school graduate. You must be eligible for a security clearance and volunteer for airborne training. You must achieve a minimum General Aptitude (GT) test score of 110 and a combat operation score of 98 on the Armed Services Vocational Aptitude Battery. You must also complete the Defense Language Aptitude Battery or Defense Language Proficiency Test.

SF soldiers (also known as Green Berets) must be able to operate independently and without resupply in any environment. They learn to use their sense of smell and sound as well as sight. This SF student is tracking enemy movement through the jungle. Special Forces units often conduct counter drug operations in Central and South America. © Fred Pushies

Above: An SF Soldier from 10th Special Forces discusses battle tactics with African soldiers whom he must train and perhaps someday fight alongside. Many foreign soldiers may have been fighting since they were young boys. They may initially believe that the Green Berets cannot teach them anything. Special Forces soldiers know how to work with foreign armies and earn their respect and cooperation. The training at this time is land navigation, patrolling, battle drills, and assault formations.

Below: Special Forces soldiers from the 1/10th SF Group teach mounted tactics to soldiers for the Malian Army in Timbuktu. Green Berets operate in numerous North African countries to include Mali, Mauritania, Niger, and Chad. These African forces will be engaged in efforts to eliminate arms smuggling, drug trafficking, and movement of terrorists through the region. Green Berets often accompany them on operations.

"They may not be pretty, but they can fight." A Special Forces soldier in Afghanistan stands with his group of resistance fighters. The Northern Alliance tribal fighter is holding a rocket-propelled grenade launcher. These local fighters have been fighting for years and their combat skills should never be underestimated. The SF soldier will have to earn their respect if he is going to succeed in advising them. The SF soldier is armed with a submachinegun.

As you progress through training you will be expected to pass the Army Physical Fitness Test at the 17- to 21-year-old standard, with a minimum score of 229 and at least 60 points in each event. Also, you will have to pass the Special Forces swim test. Your swimming ability will first be evaluated during Phase Ib, known as the Special Forces Assessment and Selection (SFAS) phase. Plan on exceeding the minimums.

Upon qualifying and enlisting in the Army for the Special Forces training program, you are only guaranteed that you have an admissions pass for each phase of the training. Of course, if you fail any phase of training, the admission ticket is canceled. At any point in which you fail a phase or course, you are "washed

out" and reassigned to whatever military unit and specialty that the Army may need filled.

The John F. Kennedy Special Warfare Center at Fort Bragg, North Carolina, is the "schoolhouse" and has established twelve personal attributes associated with the successful completion of Special Forces training. The first two, *intelligence* and *physical fitness* are objective requirements that will be measured in academic and physical testing. The next ten are subjective, and at every step of the training process the Army will look for evidence of these character traits in you. This book will look at all of them and provide actual examples as to why they are so important to the success of Special Forces missions. The critical twelve traits are illustrated through brief glimpses into training or combat missions as told by Green Berets.

TRAIT #1: INTELLIGENCE

Whether a Special Forces soldier is calling in an artillery strike that must account for the curvature of the earth, discussing the historic hierarchy of elderly people in an ancient village, or calculating the optimum location and quantity of explosives to bring down a bridge, he will have to accomplish all of these tasks with insight and precision. Special Forces soldiers must have a good grasp of physics, geometry, language construction, history, political groups, agriculture, and economics.

Green Berets must be intelligent enough to grasp complex technology and be adept at intellectually evaluating such obscure factors as the impact of environmental, cultural, and religious influences in their operational area.

TRAIT #2: PHYSICAL FITNESS

"One night we made a static-line jump into a mountainous area where the drop zone was at an 8,000-foot elevation. Our aircraft was flying at 900 feet above ground level. Each team member carried a full rucksack with an average weight well over 100 pounds. The temperature at drop time was about 80 degrees. The high altitude and warm temperature made the air very thin. We descended fast. I struck the ground like a falling brick. Another team member hit a power line and was burned, but he was OK. We had to evacuate the drop zone quickly.

A Special Forces Soldier conducts Security Assistance Training for members of the Philippine Armed Forces. The training was held on the Zamboanga Peninsula of the Philippine Islands. This is a classic SF Counter Terrorist mission. SF soldiers are often in situations where there is no field manual and no superior commanders to consult. They must be able to exercise mature judgment at all times.

Special Forces soldiers are often in some of the most dangerous combat situations. It is not uncommon for them to have earned medals for heroism, but their heroic actions often go unnoticed as they operate independently and behind enemy lines. On this occasion their actions were noticed. Lieutenant General Philip R. Kensinger Jr. awards decorations for valor during combat operations to members of the "Desert Eagles" (1st Battalion, 3rd Special Forces Group). The 3rd Special Forces Group infiltrated early into Afghanistan, and as that war wound down they deployed directly into combat in Iraq. Both of these SF soldiers have just received the Silver Star. The NCO in the foreground is also receiving a Purple Heart.

"For quite some time we also carried our main and reserve parachutes. Later we buried the chutes. Additionally, we carried 5-gallon water cans for every two team members. Responsibility for carrying the water was alternated between each pair of soldiers every 15 minutes. We moved all night through ravines, jagged rocks, and thick brush, and we scaled steep cliffs. At one point, just a few feet from cresting the top of a very steep cliff, there was hardly an ounce of energy left in any of us. I recall thinking that it was easier to imagine falling hundreds of feet to certain death than it was to imagine one more pull upwards. Our bodies were trembling with exhaustion and pain."

Special Forces missions require physical fitness *and exceptional stamina.*

TRAIT #3: MOTIVATION

"My team had been living in the mountains for about 10 days, conducting reconnaissance of the target area. Our mission was to infiltrate the city below and seize the local radio station. We were to capture the propaganda minister alive and conduct a brief broadcast

At any given time, Special Forces soldiers are on assignments in more than 100 countries around the world. In this picture, a soldier from the Republic of Georgia is flanked by a Green Beret officer and NCO assigned to the 10th Special Forces Group, which has primary responsibility for the Eastern Europe area. The 10th Group had been training for many months inside the former Soviet state.

The Special Forces unit crest is worn by all SF soldiers on their dress green uniform. SF enlisted men also wear the crest fastened over the Group Flash on their beret. The crest features the V42 fighting knife, which was a weapon of choice by the First Special Service Force in World War II. This dagger overlayed on a pair of crossed arrows represents the silent and deadly weapons used by the American Indians. The scroll *De Oppresso Liber* is the SF motto expressed in Latin: to liberate the oppressed.
© Hans Halberstadt

19

to the population. After that we were to render the station and transmission tower inoperable, and exfiltrate.

"To get into the city, we loaded into the back of two horse trailers owned by local ranchers that were assisting our team. The trailers were fitted with false floors, and we slid into the space underneath and in between the two floors. Horses were then walked into each trailer. In my trailer, we had a stallion on top of us. A thin layer of hay covered the floor. On the way into the city an enemy checkpoint halted our group. While one of the guards was peering into the back of our trailer, the horse discharged his bladder and we were treated to an unexpected shower through the cracks in the false floor.

"In the city, we met up with some local supporters at a safe house. After dark they drove us in their vehicles toward the target while we lay flat in the back of their cars. The radio station was situated in the center of a farm field about 2 kilometers from where we would exit the vehicles. Our transportation slowed but could not be seen to stop. One by one we rolled out and bounced down the gravel road and into a stinking drainage ditch.

"We began moving toward the target. It would take several hours to low crawl the distance to the station. The farm field was covered in 5 or 6 inches of water and muck. It was a cold night and the water was bone chilling. The area was surrounded with enemy guard patrols. As I dragged my body, face in the mud, crawling as low as possible toward the station, I occasionally encountered a warm spot. I paused and enjoyed the warmth. It was very comforting, until I realized that those warm spots in the shallow water were recent droppings from nearby farm animals.

"We initiated our attack. The entire city woke up from the gunfire and explosions. Afterwards, we moved cross country for hours toward a farm from which we would be extracted by chopper at dawn. Enemy soldiers were frantically searching everywhere for us. We reached the farm and hid out in a multistory chicken coop for several hours while we waited for the helicopters. I was totally exhausted. There were noisy chickens above me and they, like the horse, also had periodic discharges. I was too tired to care."

There is often nothing glamorous about a Special Forces mission. Simply wanting to wear the famed "Green Beret" will fall far short of the requirement to be motivated.

A Special Forces sniper team is positioned on a rooftop. An MH-6 "Little Bird" helicopter hovers in the background with back-up forces to assist the sniper team. Many Special Forces students will also attend Sniper School. Those who do will train the rest of their team in sniper skills. This is known as "train the trainer," a concept used on all Special Forces Operational Detachments. Cross-training is a never-ending process for Green Berets.

A Special Forces soldier leaps from a UH-60 Black Hawk helicopter high above central Alaska. This will be a high-altitude low-opening parachute jump. Special Forces soldiers frequently infiltrate target areas using free-fall techniques. On this jump, the soldier will free fall for about 10,000 feet before deploying his parachute. However, sometimes Special Forces soldiers will jump from much higher altitudes with oxygen and deploy their parachutes immediately following their exit.

TRAIT #4: TRUSTWORTHINESS

"We were operating as a split team. We had completed our primary reconnaissance mission and were now cutting through mountains, headed toward our extraction point. We were in a remain-over-night [RON] position and it was nearing the time to send a burst transmission to headquarters. The technique, known as "bursting", condenses what would otherwise be a lengthy radio message into a very short transmission that will move rapidly across the airwaves as a small compact and encoded package. Bursting reduces possible detection and intercept by enemy units. As the team radio operator, I would have to distance myself from the team before transmitting the message. If I remained too close to the team's location, and my transmission was intercepted by the enemy, I could endanger the entire team. The enemy would surely send air strikes or artillery in on top of us. I headed out. The terrain I had to cross to achieve significant separation from the team was daunting. After I transmitted the message I had to return over the same ground. No one on my team will ever know if I sent the message from 1 klick [kilometer] or 15 klicks away. They trust me, and I will never let them down." *At all times, Green Berets must be* trustworthy.

A group of special forces students at the U.S. Army Combat Divers Qualification Course wade into the south Atlantic waters off Key West, Florida. They are about to begin a daylight underwater navigation, search, and recovery exercise. This is just the beginning of many complex and physically exhausting underwater operations. More than anything else, they will be tested in their ability to maintian composure and demonstrate clear thinking during critical underwater situations.

TRAIT #5: ACCOUNTABILITY

"It was an intense firefight. One of our team members mistakenly shot an unarmed civilian who was headed toward our position in the darkness. It would have been difficult, if not impossible, to determine who fired the shot that killed the wrong person. Later, during an inquiry, there was no hesitation on the part of the team member who had shot the man: He accepted complete responsibility." *Regardless of the potential consequences, Special Forces soldiers must hold themselves* accountable *for their actions.*

TRAIT #6: MATURITY

"Our team was living with a tribe whose tradition required that a young man of approximately 13 years of age, as a rite of passage through puberty, must have his front teeth knocked out in a ceremonial ritual. We participated in the ceremony and congratulated the young man. None of our team members would have ever considered joking, laughing, or mocking this cultural ritual . . . not even privately, among ourselves." *Green Berets must demonstrate* maturity *in their interaction with other peoples, cultures, and religions.*

Special Forces soldiers conduct a dismounted assault from a Humvee (High Mobility, Multipurpose, Wheeled Vehicle, or HMMWV). Many specially modified Humvees are referred to as Ground Mobility Vehicles. They are so vastly modified as to have only a slight resemblance to the original Humvee. This vehicle is equipped with a .50-caliber machine gun.

TRAIT #7: STABILITY

"As the night battle raged, the sheer number of enemy soldiers began to overwhelm us. Some of our team members were engaged in hand-to-hand combat, and others found that their machine gun barrels were melting down from the constant rapid firing. Wounded local militia soldiers were all around us, screaming. Team members were shouting to one another. RPGs were exploding around us.

"On the radio were friendly aircraft asking where to drop their bombs. Also on the radio were artillery units, asking what fire adjustments were required. An Air Force forward controller insisted that I provide the technical data to establish an imaginary corridor in the sky so that his aircraft could safely pass without the risk of being hit by friendly artillery. The fighter jets on station were running low on fuel and had just minutes left to drop their bombs or leave the battle area. They needed targets identified and friendly positions marked. Medical evacuation chopper pilots were asking me to identify a landing zone so they could extract our seriously wounded.

A member of the 1st Special Forces Group exits the tailgate of a C7 Caribou at about 1,000 feet above ground level (AGL) in Australia. They are working with the Australian Special Air Service (SAS) based on the West Coast, near the city of Perth. The SAS are Australia's version of our Special Forces. This is a static-line jump off the back ramp, which on this aircraft has a seven-degree downward slope. On a C7, once the jump "train" gets moving toward the back ramp, there is no slowing down the forward momentum. Jump procedures for various types of aircraft are slightly different. Special Forces jumpmasters are constantly reviewing and updating spotting, control, and exit techniques as they train with armies from around the world.

Left: A Special Forces officer awards United States airborne wings to Canadian and North African soldiers in Edmonton, Alberta, Canada. Special Forces personnel are continuously engaged in military cross-training with other countries. On this occasion, SF personnel were trained in Canadian airborne operations while simultaneously the 3rd Battalion, 12th Special Forces Group trained members of the Canadian Defense Force Parachute Regiment and their allies in U.S. airborne operations. *CWO James Gaston*

Right: The Special Forces shoulder sleeve insignia or unit patch, as it is often called, symbolizes the heritage of Special Forces. It is worn by all soldiers assigned to a Special Forces unit regardless of whether or not they have completed Special Forces training. All personnel assigned to a Special Forces unit must be airborne-qualified so a gold-on-black airborne tab worn above the arrowhead is a basic component of the SF unit patch. The shape of the patch is an arrowhead that represents the American Indian's special skills, many of which are learned and practiced by SF. The upturned dagger, or fighting knife, represents the unconventional nature of Special Forces missions. The three lightening bolts symbolize the Green Beret's ability to strike rapidly by land, sea, or air. *Photo © Hans Halberstadt.*

"Just then, several enemy soldiers popped up within a few feet of me and leaped over the sandbags into our fighting position. After we took care of the interruption, I returned to the radio and continued to establish the artillery corridor, direct the medical evacuation chopper, and issue the orders to mark our position with directional strobes. I then prioritized the myriad of support aircraft that were offering assistance." *Mental stability under intense stress is a must for a Green Beret.*

TRAIT #8: JUDGMENT

"We caught the enemy fighters by complete surprise. We surrounded them inside a small village. This enemy unit was accountable for many attacks on our base camp. We had finally caught up with them. Suddenly, from the doorways of the buildings came enemy soldiers who shielded themselves with women and children. Many of these women and children were their own wives, sons, and daughters. They walked directly in front and past us. It was a difficult judgment call as to what to do next." *Green Berets are often confronted with situations that require sound judgment.*

TRAIT #9: DECISIVENESS

"Our boat chopped through the swells at top speed. We were heading into the target area. Our missile-launch detection equipment gave off an alarm that an enemy missile had a radar lock on our boat. An unidentified incoming aircraft appeared on the screen. I suspected it to be enemy but was uncertain. If I fired the surface-to-air missile and I was wrong—that is, if the aircraft turned out to be nonhostile—I would likely have killed innocent people and exposed our team. If I didn't fire the missile, my men might have died within the next few seconds." *Decisiveness can be the difference between life and death.*

TRAIT #10: TEAMWORK

"During the fight our team communications sergeant was patching up a sucking chest wound and our engineer and our weapons sergeant set up the medical triage before the doc got there. Our team members know one another so well that we can often predict each other's thoughts. We cross-train each of our basic skill sets with at least one other team member. No one on the team would ever think of saying, 'That's not my job.' We do whatever it takes to make the team successful. It's the synergy of our efforts that produces results which are greater than the sum of our 12 men." *How well a man can work as a team member is critical to the success of any Special Forces mission.*

TRAIT #11: INFLUENCE

"The foreign soldiers and local freedom fighters that we were sent to train did not greet us with open arms. They were suspicious of our intentions, reluctant to change their old methods, and would not respond to orders. If we were going to go into battle with them against a well-trained enemy force, we had better know a thing or two about winning their hearts and minds and convincing them that there is a better way." *The ability to influence others to do what they would not normally do is an essential characteristic of all Green Berets.*

TRAIT #12: COMMUNICATIONS

"During a particularly tense moment in the fighting, as the enemy closed in on us, I shouted to one of the local fighters in his native language, 'Fix bayonets!' and he responded that his was not broken. He took the word *fix*

Teamwork applies to every challenge an ODA encounters. The communications sergeant may find himself assisting with surgery or the team medic may have to assist the engineer clearing a minefield. Even in the officer ranks there are no prima donnas on an ODA. In this photo, SF team members treat their wounded indigenous fighters while plans for continuing the operation are being discussed in the background.

Conducting military operations in extreme cold weather conditions is an essential part of Special Forces training at the Army's Northern Operations Training Center in Delta, Alaska. This SF soldier is navigating with a global positioning system. When operating near the poles, magnetic compasses can be difficult if not impossible to use. Photo © Fred Pushies

literally as meaning 'to repair.' We also discovered that our local fighters were confused by our term *lock and load*. In still another country we discovered that the local people had no words for military technology. For example, there was no direct translation for the word *helicopter*. The words they used for helicopter were *my-by-whop-whop*, translated to [mean] a bird that makes a whop, whop sound!" *In all military operations it is necessary to be clear, concise, and understood. Green Berets must be especially able to communicate effectively at all levels with all people.*

On your path toward becoming a Green Beret, recruiters, guidance counselors, suitability review boards, instructors, and even fellow students will observe your strengths and weaknesses in these 12 areas. To become a Special Forces soldier you will need to consistently demonstrate these character traits. Your decisions and your actions must reflect these traits as innate characteristics of your personality.

It takes an enlisted man one to two years to earn his "license to practice," the Special Forces tab. There are 10 hurdles in the quest to be a Green Beret: (1) Basic Training, (2) Advanced Individual Training, (3) Airborne School, (4) Army Common Leadership Training (ACLT), and the six phases of the Special Forces Qualification Course (SFQC), often called the Q course.

Officers who hope to achieve Special Forces Qualification need to complete (1) the commissioning program (Military Academy, Reserve Officer Training Course, or the Officer Candidate Course), (2) the Officer Basic Course, (3) Airborne School, (4) the Officer Advance Course, and the six phases of SFQC.

The ACLT requirement for enlisted men, which is just a few weeks long, is called the Primary Leadership Development Course/Basic Non-Commissioned Officers Course (PLDC/BNCOC). Officers may need as long as nine months to complete the Officers Advance Course. Phase II begins after completion of ACLT, and the remainder of the Q course will be about six months for most students. Medic and communications specialty courses take the longest. For example, the Special Forces Medical Training phase is nearly a year long by itself. Also, the specific language training to which you are assigned could extend training time by many months.

By now you should clearly see that Special Forces *is not* a hat, it *is not* a tab, it *is not* a qualification badge, and it *is not* an assignment. It is a commitment to attaining extraordinary knowledge and skills and employing those skills in the military world's most challenging and dangerous assignments. Only those men with incredible determination, self-discipline, and focus make it through the Q course.

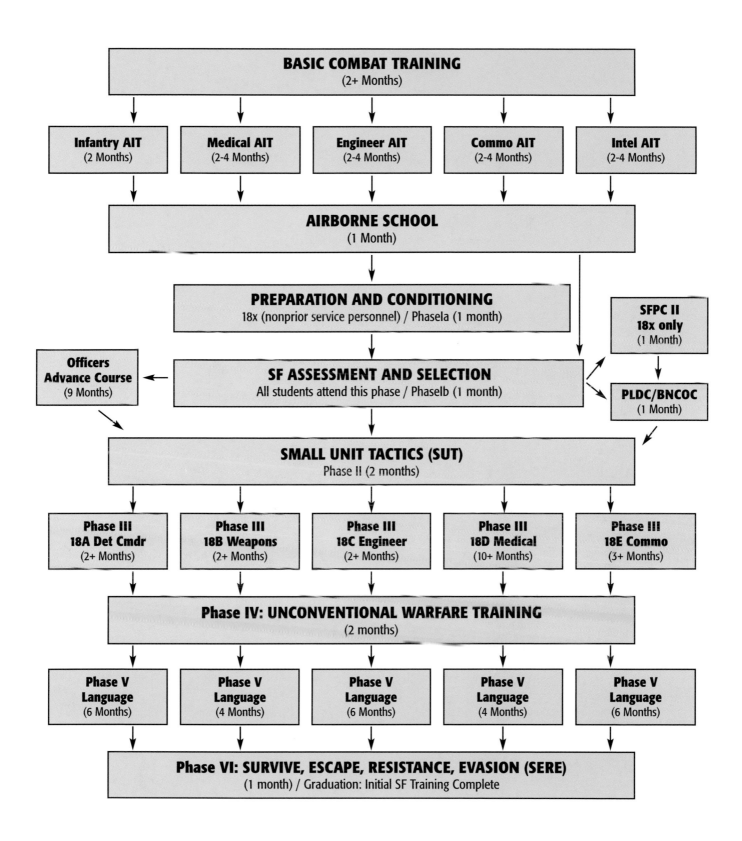

BASIC COMBAT TRAINING
(2+ Months)

Infantry AIT
(2 Months)

Medical AIT
(2-4 Months)

Engineer AIT
(2-4 Months)

Commo AIT
(2-4 Months)

Intel AIT
(2-4 Months)

AIRBORNE SCHOOL
(1 Month)

PREPARATION AND CONDITIONING
18x (nonprior service personnel) / Phasela (1 month)

SFPC II
18x only
(1 Month)

Officers
Advance Course
(9 Months)

SF ASSESSMENT AND SELECTION
All students attend this phase / Phaselb (1 month)

PLDC/BNCOC
(1 Month)

SMALL UNIT TACTICS (SUT)
Phase II (2 months)

Phase III
18A Det Cmdr
(2+ Months)

Phase III
18B Weapons
(2+ Months)

Phase III
18C Engineer
(2+ Months)

Phase III
18D Medical
(10+ Months)

Phase III
18E Commo
(3+ Months)

Phase IV: UNCONVENTIONAL WARFARE TRAINING
(2 months)

Phase V
Language
(6 Months)

Phase V
Language
(4 Months)

Phase V
Language
(6 Months)

Phase V
Language
(4 Months)

Phase V
Language
(6 Months)

Phase VI: SURVIVE, ESCAPE, RESISTANCE, EVASION (SERE)
(1 month) / Graduation: Initial SF Training Complete

BLUEPRINT FOR CHANGE

It is said that the best battle plan survives only the first five minutes of contact. After those first five minutes, the side that demonstrates the greatest flexibility often wins. In that same vein, Special Forces soldiers must be flexible, and, by extension, Special Forces training must be flexible. While fundamental concepts must be maintained and reinforced, the Special Forces training curriculum is not a stagnant concept. Battlefield lessons are quickly incorporated into the training of the next generation of Special Forces soldiers. Improvements in instructional methods are continually made; this process must be quicker and more efficient than the enemy's efforts to do the same. As this book goes to press, the Army's Special Warfare Training Group has developed a "Blueprint for Change" intended to update and improve the curriculum and sequence of classes in the current "Q" course.

Special Forces Group assignments, each soldier's area orientation, and language requirements will be known at the beginning of a student's Special Forces training. Phase II will include Peacetime Governmental Detention/Hostage Detention, intended to improve the handling of prisoners—a contentious subject in recent times. Phase V (proposed to be the new Phase IV) will still focus on languages, but language training will also be incorporated as modularized classes throughout the "Q" course. One advantage of this will be challenging students to use foreign language abilities and demonstrate cultural awareness during field exercises, most notably in the Robin Sage exercise of the Unconventional Warfare phase. Another benefit is that the Language phase may be reduced in length due to the earlier introduction of modularized language classes.

The blueprint for change proposes that Survival, Escape, Resistance, and Evasion (SERE) should become a component of all the phases and receive the greatest emphasis during the Small Unit Tactics/Common Skills phase. As these changes are implemented, SERE will not be a separate phase—this will shorten the "Q" course but not materially affect the content. The course will be streamlined to reduce wait time between phases. Other additions include intelligence collection, abduction avoidance, captivity survival, and adaptive thinking. An exciting proposed change that is undergoing a "pilot" test, is sending students to the desert at Fort Irwin, California, near Death Valley. This immerses students in regionally oriented, language, and cultural awareness training while simulating a combat environment.

Some of the planned changes will become institutionalized, while others may not survive the test of time. The proposed changes will not change the essence of Special Forces training. Except as previously mentioned, SFQC fundamentally remains the same program that has consistently produced the finest warriors in world: U.S. Army Green Berets. Under the proposed changes:

· Language training will become Phase IV and Unconventional Warfare training will become Phase V. The change is intended to allow students to practice their foreign language capabilities while interfacing with resistance force role players during the Robin Sage exercise.

· The wearing of the Green Beret, issuance of the Group coin, and Regimental dinner will not take place until Phase VI, which will appropriately be called "Regimental First Formation & Graduation."

· Finally, the Special Warfare Center is planning on eliminating the Survival, Escape, Resistance, and Evasion (SERE) phase and integrating the same training into Phase II, Small Unit Tactics and Common Skills training.

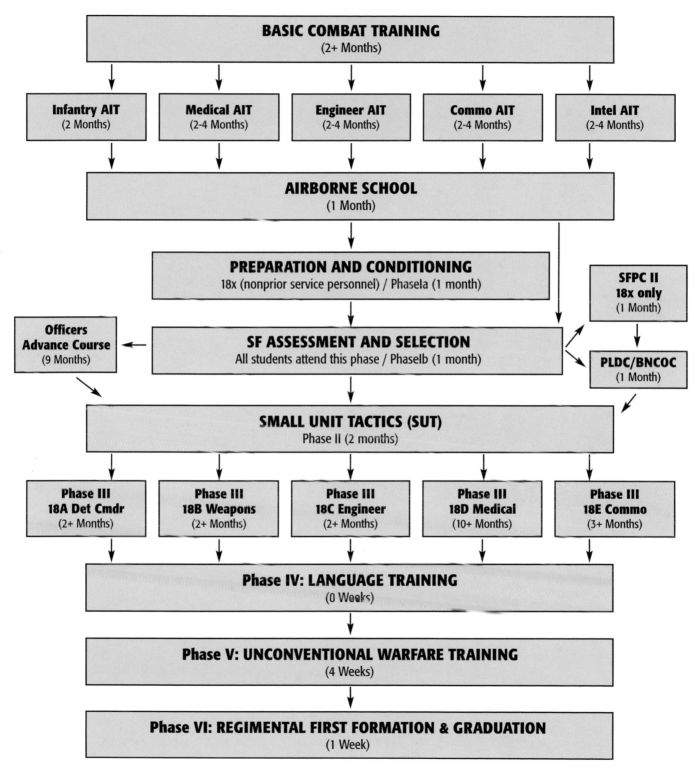

BASIC COMBAT TRAINING
(2+ Months)

| **Infantry AIT**
(2 Months) | **Medical AIT**
(2-4 Months) | **Engineer AIT**
(2-4 Months) | **Commo AIT**
(2-4 Months) | **Intel AIT**
(2-4 Months) |

AIRBORNE SCHOOL
(1 Month)

PREPARATION AND CONDITIONING
18x (nonprior service personnel) / Phasela (1 month)

SFPC II
18x only
(1 Month)

Officers Advance Course
(9 Months)

SF ASSESSMENT AND SELECTION
All students attend this phase / Phaselb (1 month)

PLDC/BNCOC
(1 Month)

SMALL UNIT TACTICS (SUT)
Phase II (2 months)

| **Phase III**
18A Det Cmdr
(2+ Months) | **Phase III**
18B Weapons
(2+ Months) | **Phase III**
18C Engineer
(2+ Months) | **Phase III**
18D Medical
(10+ Months) | **Phase III**
18E Commo
(3+ Months) |

Phase IV: LANGUAGE TRAINING
(0 Weeks)

Phase V: UNCONVENTIONAL WARFARE TRAINING
(4 Weeks)

Phase VI: REGIMENTAL FIRST FORMATION & GRADUATION
(1 Week)

TWO

NBC (Nuclear, Biological, and Chemical) defense training is incorporated at every level of a soldier's schooling. In Basic Combat Training soldiers are exposed to tear gas and they learn to properly put on a mask within 9 seconds. In AIT soldiers will actually conduct operations while masked and outfitted in a protective suit known as MOPP gear (Mission Oriented Protective Posture).

The Training Road Map

The process of entering the Army begins at the local recruiting station. This experience, as you will discover, is somewhat deceptive. Commonly, the recruiter is a staff sergeant, a noncommissioned officer (NCO). You will probably call him by his first name: Mike, for example. He is probably a very friendly sort of guy. You may even meet Mike's boss who is a captain, a commissioned officer, and he might introduce himself as John, or whatever. Don't get too cozy in this love fest with NCOs and officers. When you arrive at your basic training post, don't even think about speaking to a staff sergeant or captain as you did Mike or John. If you think you are going to chit-chat with the staff sergeant at your basic training post, he'll eat you for breakfast. And as to running into a captain, like John, you're not likely to get within a hundred yards of a captain and, if you do, you will be frozen at attention.

A Basic Training soldier negotiates a simulated rope bridge while working through an obstacle course. In nearly every Army combat training school, students will encounter an obstacle course. The complexity increases at each level of training. This one is about 100 yards long with six stations (obstacles). Later, in Special Forces training, the course will be nearly 2 miles long with far more obstacles and requiring much more strength and agility.

A drill sergeant demonstrates right and left shoulder arms to a group of trainees. Today's training includes military movements such as the position of attention, parade rest, present arms, right and left face, about face, and at ease. All of these moves are practiced with and without a weapon. Proper military bearing is required at all times. Drill sergeants epitomize these qualities and instill them in their trainees.

BASIC TRAINING

Basic training is eight weeks of learning how and who to salute, how to march, to fire a rifle, to administer first aid, to put on a gas mask, to check the air for chemical agents, to negotiate an obstacle course, to experience bullets and explosions around you, to learn the difference between fire-and-movement and fire-and-maneuver, to get into good physical condition, and to get over your family and your neighborhood separation anxiety. You are in the Army now. Get over it and get with it!

You will probably think your drill sergeant is not a product of natural birth. He must have been manufactured in some military laboratory, deep underground. He will seem more like an insensitive machine that has no grasp on how hard this is on poor you. Oh, he knows. And more important, he knows what training it takes to keep men alive in combat.

You will now have your first opportunity to begin to develop, build, and demonstrate the character traits required to be a Green Beret. Opportunities to be a student squad leader, platoon leader, or first sergeant will be available. More is expected of those student leaders than the rank-and-file trainees. Special Forces applicants would do well to pursue these leadership positions.

A drill sergeant inspects a Basic Training soldier's gear. Basic is an eight-week program that covers physical fitness, proper wear and care of military uniform and equipment, marching drills, military courtesy, rifle marksmanship, basic first aid, field craft, chemical and biological defense, military justice, general orders for all soldiers, and fundamentals of responding under enemy fire.

"Follow me, I am infantry" bellows out the age-old cadence song at Fort Benning, Georgia. The unit guidon (flag) of this Advanced Individual Training Group (AIT) displays the infantry school patch. These soldiers have completed Basic Training, and when they complete infantry AIT most will be assigned to the Army's front line combat units. For every one infantry fighter in the Army, there are more than a dozen soldiers who serve in a support role to these combat soldiers. © Hans Halberstadt

These soldiers are graduating from Basic. Their drill sergeant stands in the foreground in his green dress uniform. Soldiers can glean much of this NCO's experience with a simple glance at his uniform. He has fought in ground combat, he is Ranger-qualified, a master parachutist, completed the air assault school, an expert marksman, served in the Gulf War, and received many decorations, including a Bronze Star.

ADVANCE INDIVIDUAL TRAINING

As a Special Forces applicant you should be in a Military Occupational Specialties (MOS) that is especially useful to Special Forces. This is infantry, artillery, combat engineering, communications, medical, or intelligence. Depending on which school you are in, your course will probably be somewhere from eight to sixteen weeks.

AIRBORNE SCHOOL

"Anyone can fall out of a perfectly good airplane." It takes a highly trained and skilled professional to do it from a jet, at 140 knots, at night, loaded down with a main parachute, a reserve parachute, a full rucksack, and a weapon, with jumpers exiting out of two doors simultaneously and joining 200 other jumpers in the air. It takes more than that to be aware of and instinctively respond to any mid-air problems and land safely. It takes a graduate of the Army's Airborne School.

So you thought your drill sergeant in Basic was the meanest mother in the valley. Obviously, you never met a "Black Hat." You will now. Welcome to the 1st Battalion 507th Infantry Regiment. This is the Airborne School Student Training Battalion at Fort Benning, Georgia. "Airborne!" "How far?" "All the way!" is your battle cry. Say it in your sleep and mean it! This three-week training program will seem as long as your eight

A "Black Hat" inquires as to what might be the "major maladjustment" of a student. The lieutenant in the background appears to be a student leader, but he enjoys no special privilege with regard to treatment. His rank is merely a convenience for the benefit of class control. The black hats send officers into the sawdust pit for pushups just as frequently as they do enlisted men. "Get down and knock out 50—sir!"

An airborne student practices his exit technique through the "mock door." Two of the most important aspects to experiencing a safe jump are to exit correctly and land correctly. The landing part is called a Parachute Landing Fall (PLF). These two skills will be practiced a thousand times before the end of the three-week training program. They must become instinctive responses for the airborne soldier.

Left: Jumpers exit a C-130 Turbo Prop. Notice as the jumper falls, his feet begin rising. This can be partially due to the prop blast and the vertical wind shear. He must maintain that tight body position until his chute opens. If he looks up to see his chute before it is fully open, he will likely get *riser burns* behind his ears. Once on the ground, Airborne soldiers love to poke fun at a jumper who has a few drops of blood just behind the ear. "What's a matter, Joe . . . did you panic thinkin' your chute wasn't gonna open?" *© Hans Halberstadt*

Right: This parachutist descends from the sky in a T-10 chute. The way you can tell it is a T-10 is that the chute has no holes in the sides for airflow. It is not very maneuverable and parachutists must pull hard on their riser straps to cause the chute to move in one direction or another. For mass tactical jumps, where hundreds of parachutists are in the sky at once, the military prefers this type of canopy. The reason: everyone is coming straight down and they don't want to have a lot of folks banging into one another. This jumper has released his rucksack on the lower line and he is preparing to land by "holding into the wind." *© Hans Halberstadt*

Students are hooked up to the anchor line cable. If you look closely you can see the jumpmaster's hand on the door. He is leaning far outside of the aircraft and watching for the drop zone and checking for other aircraft. In a moment, he will pop back inside, turn and look at this first jumper, and command, "Stand in the door."

weeks in basic training. You will get tougher every day. The stuff you thought was impossible in Basic is now routine. You will learn every conceivable emergency response, and you will execute it instinctively upon experiencing any given potential malfunction. You will even learn how to safely get off of another parachutist's canopy and reinflate your chute while you both descend. These response mechanisms will be so ingrained in you that you will be capable of surviving any condition you might encounter while exiting an airplane in flight. The Black Hats will make certain of that. The three weeks of airborne school consist of ground week, tower week, and jump week.

In ground week you will learn the jump command sequence, door-exit positions, and proper exit method when leaving various types of aircraft. You will practice these sequences by jumping from a 34-foot structure that lets you out onto a pulley-guided cable.

In tower week, the training will concentrate on parachute landing falls and control of the parachute during descent. During this week you will experience devices called "suspended agony," the swing landing trainer, and the wind machine. You will also be hauled up a tower by cable in a pre-opened parachute and released. In between all of this, you will do never-ending series of pushups in the sawdust pit.

In jump week you will conduct five jumps from a combination of turbo-prop and jet aircraft. Sitting in the aircraft you are about to respond to the jump command sequence for real. The airplane doors will be raised and opened. Your senses will be overwhelmed by the wind whipping inside the aircraft, the smell of jet fuel, the perspiration pouring off the faces of you and your fellow students, the droning engine noise, and your apprehension (apprehension is also known as controlled fear). The jumpmaster will position himself in the rear center of the aircraft and begin giving arm-and-hand signals while shouting out the jump commands:

"Get ready!"
"Outboard personnel stand up!"
"Inboard personnel stand up!"
"Hook up!"
"Check static line!"
"Check equipment!"
"Sound off for equipment check!"

Airborne students sit in the ready area at Lawson Army Airfield, waiting to board their aircraft for the final jump prior to graduation. The first couple of jumps are "Hollywood," that is, with a helmet, main, and reserve chute only. These last jumps are full-equipment jumps, including a packed rucksack and rifle.

Future paratroopers on their morning run. In the background are the swing landing trainers and lateral drift apparatus where students practice parachute landing falls over and over and over. All across Fort Benning one can hear the morning shrill of airborne students singing, "C-130 rolling down the strip, airborne daddy gonna take a little trip. Stand up, hook up, shuffle to the door, jump right out and count to four. If my shoot don't open wide, I got another one by my side; if that one should fail me too, look out clouds, I'm comin' through." © Hans Halberstadt

During the first week in Airborne School, also called "Ground Week," students will practice jumps from a 34-foot-high platform while hooked to a cable line that, following your jump, slides on a pulley mechanism parallel to the ground for about 50 yards. After exiting the platform and counting to four, the student looks up to simulate checking his parachute. Randomly, the line above the jumper may have a small red flag, which indicates that the jumper's chute has malfunctioned. The jumper must then replicate all the proper procedures for initiating deployment of the reserve parachute.

The second week of Airborne School is often called "tower week." In this photo you can see two of the three 250-foot towers. Students, suspended underneath a parachute, are hauled up to the top by a cable. They are released and float down. They must pull the correct "slips" so as not to float into the tower and execute a proper PLF on impact. © Hans Halberstadt

Your jumpmaster will lean far out the door of the aircraft. He'll pop back in and extend his arm toward you while raising up his forefinger as he shouts, "One minute!" A few moments later he will stare into the face of the first student and bellow out, "Stand in the door!" Standing in the door will seem like an eternity, but only seconds will have passed by the time you hear a loud "GO!" This is the moment of truth.

The "train" of jumpers begins the airborne shuffle toward the door. No one is going to stop. This line of jumpers has the momentum of a diesel locomotive plowing toward the end of the track—the open jump door.

As you exit the airplane you will be surprised by the force of the wind that smacks you. Your feet will start to rise. You'll hear the soft *pop, pop, pop* of your static line and deployment bag breaking the rubber bands and strings that were used in the packing of the chute. Your chute is pulling open and you feel the initial opening shock. Unless you had a perfect exit, there's a good chance you will have some twists in your suspension lines. You will bicycle out your twist like you were trained to do the previous week.

Your chute will pop open farther. Now you have a completely open canopy over your head. For just a moment you may find yourself thanking God or someone else. Maybe you'll thank the Black Hat you thought you hated. In that same moment you will be struck by the contrast from the noise and tension that was inside the aircraft, which has now turned into serene silence as you float down in the sky. Don't congratulate yourself yet. You still have to safely land that ball of silk. But you are well on your way to becoming "Airborne."

The C-130 aircraft is a workhorse that is often used by all airborne soldiers, including Special Forces. It can hold up to 60 jumpers (about 40 fully combat-equipped). Airborne soldiers can exit out both doors simultaneously or jumpers can exit off the back ramp.

A Fort Benning AIT soldier runs to his next firing position while covered by another soldier in the lane. This leapfrog technique is called "fire and movement." When a larger group of soldiers covers for another group that may be sweeping around the flank of the enemy it is called "fire and maneuver."

A soldier works his way over a ravine, hand over hand. This type of training is most often found in the combat arms Advance Individual Training programs. Many of these training concepts are part of the common skills required in Special Forces. Soldiers applying to Special Forces who have completed infantry, armor, or artillery AIT will have an edge over their peers.

Upon graduation from Airborne School, students are awarded their jump wings. The badge in the above photo are basic level wings. Additional rigorous training and a whole bunch more jumps are required to get the senior wings with a star on top of the parachute. The master wings with a star and a wreath surrounding the star are the highest attainable level for static-line jumping. © Hans Halberstadt

SPECIAL FORCES QUALIFICATION COURSE

PHASE IA: PREPARATION AND CONDITIONING

Phase Ia is a little more than three weeks of developing your land navigation skills and physical fitness levels so that on entry into Phase Ib, the *selection* phase, you will not experience the shock effect of going from a hot tub to an ice bath.

PHASE IB: SPECIAL FORCES ASSESSMENT AND SELECTION

That which doesn't kill you will make you stronger. You're going to believe from the depths of your soul that they *are* trying to kill you. In reality, they are just trying to reduce the number of soldiers that would otherwise "wash out" of the Q course. The Army wants the graduates of SFAS to have a high probability of making it through the Special Forces Qualification Course.

SFAS consists of land navigation exercises, runs, road marches, rappelling, and obstacle courses. You will experience sleep deprivation, physical and mental stress, and suitability evaluations. All of this is intended to determine your trainability and suitability for the Special Forces Qualification Course. At times, you are going to feel like you were sucked into a dark hole in space.

Your previous training has helped get you here, but you will now face an exponential increase in mental and physical stress management. Only your intense desire and excellent physical condition, coupled with your vivid imagination, has prepared you for this moment. Successfully completing this course requires that you have already challenged yourself with detailed mental images of the difficulty to come. To be a Green Beret you will need determination, courage, physical stamina, and an internal constitution that is founded on your original motivation for being where you are.

Left: Urban combat training, which was just a few years ago available only to special units, is now included in Advanced Individual Training.

Right: Infantry AIT includes learning how to safely and accurately employ hand grenades. This soldier and those behind him are tossing M67 "baseball" antipersonnel grenades. The casualty radius is about 15 meters or around 40 to 50 feet. This should tell you that in most cases you do not want to watch to see the results or you will be included in those results. The grenade detonates within four to five seconds after the arming lever is released, which occurs as you throw the grenade. The grenade's arming lever is depressed in the palm of the soldier's hand. It's not a good idea to fiddle with your grip once the arming lever is depressed and the pin has been pulled.

"Bang, bang, you're dead" is long obsolete! For training realism, this student is wearing MILES (Multiple Integrated Laser Engagement System). The black knobs are sensors that detect a beam from the rifles of those shooting at him, and the box on his chest triggers a high-pitched alarm signifying that he is out of action. New versions of MILES actually disable the student's rifle when he is hit so that there can be no doubt he is "down." What's more, after the battle, the cadre can download information to determine exactly who shot whom!

These soldiers are in infantry AIT and are practicing close-quarter combat drills. They will run through a series of rubber targets that must be eliminated using the butt of their weapon and the fixed bayonet attached to the front of the M16 rifle. The cadre bellows out, "What is the spirit of the bayonet?" The soldiers in chorus respond at the top of their lungs, "to kill!" The actual application of these skills in a combat situation must be confident and extremely aggressive. This training activity will ingrain the decisive behavior in each soldier. Anything less and their opponent will win the day.

During AIT, most advanced weapons training is conducted at live fire range. However, the Army has designed a wide array of simulators that will allow students to practice from the comfort of an indoor range. This example in the above photo is an AT4, antitank weapon firing a beam at a movie screen. The screen accurately registers the precise location of the hit. Practice on these simulators has clearly demonstrated improved performance at the live fire range.

Soldiers in the combat MOS AIT schools will train on increasingly more complex weapons systems. In this photo the trainee is being taught how to load and fire an M249 Squad Automatic Weapon (SAW). The SAW fires standard 5.56mm ammunition. It uses either a 30-round magazine or a 200-round box.

Phase I, Special Forces Assessment and Selection (SFAS), requires extensive physical training. The constant demands of runs, log drills, obstacle courses, land navigation, and sleep deprivation will exceed anything that a soldier may have experienced in Basic, AIT, or Airborne Training. © Hans Halberstadt.

Phase II, Small Unit Tactics, focuses on patrolling, squad and platoon movement to contact, raids, ambushes, perfecting fire and movement, marksmanship, and urban combat. You will also write and issue five-paragraph field orders. Every phase of the Q course has progressively more challenging land navigation training. © Hans Halberstadt

Phase III, Special Forces Military Occupational Specialty Training (MOS). This SF student is training to become a Special Forces weapons expert and is firing a rocket-propelled grenade launcher (RPG). Each student goes to his own individual training program that concentrates on the individual skills required of a member of a Special Forces Operational Detachment Alpha (ODA). For enlisted men the training will be either weapons, engineering, communications, or medical. Officers do not specialize in any specific skill and receive an overview of all of these areas. Much of their training concentrates on combat decision-making processes. © Hans Halberstadt

PHASE II: SMALL UNIT TACTICS

If you are entering this phase, the Army believes that you have many of the 12 attributes required of all Green Berets. Regardless of which MOS you may have, this phase is collective training for all Special Forces candidates. Over the next four weeks, you will conduct patrols, raids, ambushes, special reconnaissance, squad and platoon tactics, and a grueling 18-mile land-navigation course. The land-navigation exam is a night operation consisting of movement across miles of swamps, marsh, muck, brush, snakes, and pain.

Phase IV, Unconventional Warfare (UW). During this phase, Special Forces students will train on how to work behind enemy lines and develop civilian resistance forces into effective fighting units. The play of the problem is constantly updated to include real problems and challenges that Special Forces teams are encountering in actual current combat situations. The training exercise is known as Robin Sage. Some of the civilian role players have been helping train Green Berets on this exercise for more than 40 years. © Hans Halberstadt

PHASE III: MILITARY OCCUPATIONAL SPECIALTY (MOS) TRAINING

In this phase, each Special Forces candidate's training will concentrate on his specific specialty. The shortest is about eight weeks and the longest is nearly a year. The Special Forces specialties areas are engineering, medical, weapons, and communications. Officers attend a course of instruction that covers all of these areas in general and includes special attention on the military decision-making process. In each specialty area the training incorporates field environments building upon experience gained in the previous phase and is not exclusively classroom work.

PHASE IV: UNCONVENTIONAL WARFARE

This is where all your training truly comes together. You will operate as a member of Special Forces team in an unconventional warfare environment. Every team member will be challenged and evaluated. During the exercise, team members, without notice, will be expected to fill roles normally held by other team members. The role players in this exercise are very experienced and most are or were in Special Forces. They will employ every imaginable element of cunning to test the team's skills. Mission planning flexibility will be an integral part of this exercise. All of the 12 character traits required to be a Green Beret will be challenged and observed.

PHASE V: LANGUAGE SCHOOL

You are now wearing your Green Beret. You've spent months molding it into perfect shape: just the right angle and droop of the felt nearly touching the right ear. After the completion of Phase IV, they let you wear it. The edge seam of the beret is perfectly straight across your forehead. The Flash is perfectly positioned above your left eye. After all that you've been through, you are aching to join a Special Forces group and deploy "up country." Is this "pit stop" at language school really necessary? You bet it is.

Without a working knowledge of a foreign language, your ability to execute Special Forces missions would be seriously degraded. Depending on which foreign language course you attend, you will be in this phase for four to six months. After SFQC you might be sent to Monterey, California, to attend the Defense Language School for even further development of your language skills.

A cadre member checks out a student's web gear prior to training on the lateral drift apparatus. Students will practice "pulling slips," the act of pulling down one of the four risers to influence the direction of travel. Parachuting has many similarities to sailing. What an airborne soldier calls "crabbing" the sailor refers to as "tacking."

Left: Phase V, Language School After the first four phases of the Q course are completed, students will get a physical breather in language school. The assigned language depends on which Special Forces Group the student is assigned to and even then it will be further influenced by the Special Forces Battalion and Company assignment. For example, your group may focus on Asia but within North and Southeast Asia there are dozens of different languages, any one of which you may end up required to speak. Over the course of a career in Special Forces, Green Berets often learn to speak several different languages.
© Hans Halberstadt

A drill sergeant demonstrates the use of the M16 rifle in a hand-to-hand combat role. He is "butt stroking" and will pivot around with his body while at the same time thrusting the bayonet downward in a "slashing" movement.

PHASE VI: SURVIVAL ESCAPE AND EVASION SCHOOL (SERE)

Green Berets work in environments that place them at high risk of being captured. The SERE course trains Special Forces students on what to expect if captured, how to endure captivity, resist torture, exploit opportunities to escape, and survive for extended periods of time alone behind enemy lines. Much of this course, for good reason, is classified. During the SERE course the students—with no food, water, or weapons—will be hunted by massive numbers of role-playing enemy forces. The SERE course was originally instituted and developed by Nick Rowe, the only American soldier to escape from Viet Cong captivity during the Vietnam War. SERE has been known to break down the strongest of men.

This is the last leg in your SFQC program. On graduation, many of you will proceed on to your SF group assignments. Some of you will make a few more training pit stops before reporting to your Special Forces operational detachment Alpha.

Phase VI, Survival, Escape, Evasion and Resistance (SERE). Special Forces SERE training is a mind-bending phase that teaches students what it might be like surviving alone behind enemy lines and, if captured, how to resist the enemy. This is the final phase of the Q course before students join their SF Group.

At the completion of the SFQC, students are awarded the Special Forces tab, which will be worn on their left sleeve above the unit patch. This tab, sometimes called the "long tab," is a skill identifier representing the successful completion of SFQC and is not part of the unit patch. Therefore, it will remain on the soldier's sleeve even if the soldier's unit patch changes on future assignments.
© Hans Halberstadt

THREE

This SF student is fortunate that the dirt under the barbed wire is dry. Other obstacles on this course may be covered in 6 inches or more of water and muck. He will have to "eat dirt" to clear the low-strung barbed wire. There is no room or time for mistakes. "Low crawl" techniques of moving fast and low have to be near perfect to get through the obstacle course in the allotted time. © Hans Halberstadt

Phase Ib: Special Forces Assessment and Selection

S"Special Forces Soldiers Cannot Be Mass Produced" reads the sign at Camp Mackall, 40 miles west of Fort Bragg, North Carolina. More than 350 men stand in a circular formation listening intently to every word uttered by the cadre commander. They have just begun Phase Ib, also known as the *Selection* Phase. It is a 25-day course of instruction designed to see who will demonstrate the physical and mental qualities required to complete the remaining five phases of the Q course.

Most of these 350 physically fit, tough, fighting men who have volunteered for Special Forces are Army soldiers, but a few are Marines, Navy SEALs, or Air Force Para Rescue. Most have undergone extensive preparation for this course. Some have gone through the rigorous and physically demanding Special Forces Preparation Course. Others have focused night and day to be in top physical condition leading up to this moment. The one common denominator among them is that none is as physically or mentally ready as he thinks he is.

Some are officers, some are warrant officers, and some are senior noncommissioned officers. Some have famous brothers or fathers who have gone through this course before them. Some have seen combat. Some are paratroopers, and some are not. Some have been winners in an "iron man" competition. Some have just returned from Afghanistan or Iraq. None of that matters. None of that can be determined from looking at them or their uniforms. Nothing on their uniform identifies their previous accomplishments. Not their ranks, not even their names. What follows paraphrases the unceremonious welcome ceremony.

THE GROUND RULES

"This is a selection course," says the Special Forces cadre officer. "From here on you are a just a *number* being evaluated for acceptance into the Special Forces Training Program. You will sew your number over your nametag on your shirt and on each leg of your pants, just below the cargo pockets. No person's assessment will be influenced by who they were, what they have done, what rank you hold, what medals you have collected, or what schools you attended. We do not care.

"Most of you will not be here three weeks from now. It is not our purpose, desire, or mission to terminate your enrollment and artificially cull the ranks. To the contrary, we want to see all of you make it through the next 25 days. The Army needs Special Forces–trained men. Some of you will fail because of your inability to find your way out of the land navigation maze. A few of you will not meet the basic physical requirements. Still others will simply quit from mental or physical exhaustion. Some men will fail their peers, and some failures will result from our own psychological analysis process. The net result will be significant attrition. The best of you will be offered an opportunity to continue the process of becoming Special Forces–qualified. To make it through this training you will have to want it with all your heart, soul, and sinew. You will have to suck up internal motivation that you don't realize you have."

Unknown distance rucking occurs nearly every day during SFAS. There is no way to pace your speed because you never know how far you are going. Students just have to "suck it up" from within and draw on sheer willpower to continue. This inability to calculate how long the agony will continue replicates situations that Special Forces soldiers might encounter in combat. Anyone found carrying less than the minimum 45 pounds of weight required is immediately removed from the course. Most students will carry an extra 5 to 10 pounds rather than risk being underweight. © *Hans Halberstadt*

Special Forces Preparation Course (SFPC) Ia was formerly called SOPC (Special Operations Preparation Course). Special Forces Selection and Assessment is now Phase Ib. SFPC Ia is preparatory training for 18X (Non-Prior Service Personnel Enlisting for Special Forces). It consists of extensive physical fitness training and an introduction to land navigation. Prior service personnel proceed directly into the SFAS, Phase Ib, which is still considered by many to be the official beginning of the Q course.

In the words of one student, "In a short time I started to realize that many of these men had incredible backgrounds and, in fact, that over half of my class had already served in combat. To project such heavy student attrition among men such as these was truly intimidating. You could tell that a few would wash out fast, but the majority seemed to have the determination to die before they would fail or quit."

The Special Forces captain continued: "Unlike many other military schools, this is not a *buddy* program. During evaluation phases you will not attempt to assist another student unless specifically instructed to by a cadre. If you are caught rendering help to another student during an evaluation period, your enrollment will be terminated. You will not even provide verbal encouragement to other students. Each student must meet and pass each phase with his own internal fortitude. What you bring to the table is what you are! And that, gentlemen, is what we are here to find out."

Sergeant "O," as we will call him, typifies the diverse background of the students standing in the formation: "O" served more than 12 years in the Marine Corps prior to joining the Army and volunteering for Special Forces. He has been a combat infantry Marine and is a graduate of the famed Marine Scout-Sniper School. In addition he has completed the Marine's Amphibious Raid Course, the Navy's SCUBA school, the Jungle Survival School, and counterterrorism training with the Royal Marines. Like more than half of his class, he has seen combat—in Panama and Desert Storm. Somewhere in his military career he brushed elbows with Green Berets. He decided he had to become one, and now he too has been humbled alongside 350 other faces that are known only as numbers. Sergeant "O" is number 269.

**NAMES HAVE BEEN OMITTED
TO PROTECT IDENTITY**

The Q course students are uncomfortable with their names in print. As is common among SF, they do not want to draw unnecessary attention. These students still have a lot of training time ahead of them and they do not want the cadre to perceive them to be "grandstanders." For these reasons, most students and cadre will be referred to only as "student" or "cadre."

Camp Mackall, also known as the Colonel Nick Rowe Special Forces Training Facility, is named after one of the only Special Forces soldiers to have escaped from captivity during the Vietnam War. Over the many years he was held prisoner, the enemy began to think he was "dinky dow," which roughly translates to *crazy*. Wherever he would go he would tell his captors that he had to first start his Harley-Davidson chopper and would begin kick-starting the imaginary bike. Eventually, this helped in his escape.
© Fred Pushies

Special Forces students are generally older and more experienced than students in other Army Schools. Many will have already served in combat or are already Ranger-qualified before attending SFAS. It is not uncommon to find among the students, soldiers who previously served in other branches of the service and became attracted to Special Forces following some chance association with an A team. © Hans Halberstadt

Using a compass and map with unquestionable accuracy is as important to a Green Beret as knowing how to shoot a rifle. Special Forces soldiers will have to know how to identify their exact location on the ground under any condition, anywhere in the world. It is unacceptable to rely exclusively on global positioning systems. A person considering attending the Q course should concentrate on military map reading and physical fitness as the two most important things he can do prior to entering the course. © Hans Halberstadt

WEEK ONE
DISARMINGLY SOFT-SPOKEN

After drawing your gear, you will attend a series of informational meetings and formations. "To my surprise," said "O," "the cadre almost never yells at you. Given my previous military experience, this complete lack of screaming and shouting is truly unnerving. The cadre were more like stealth evaluators—observing, annotating, and questioning. They make notes about your number and, if you think you are beating the system with shortcuts, you may be in for a rude awakening."

Week one is full of administrative procedures, physical-fitness testing, swim evaluations, psychological testing, language-aptitude testing, and orientation on what to expect in each phase of Special Forces training.

CRAWL, WALK, RUN

Toward the end of week one, students begin to get a taste of what is to come. The entire course methodology is based on the principles of crawl, walk, and run. This means that, if you don't master all the events of week one, weeks two and three are going to be killers.

UNKNOWN DISTANCE RUNNING AND RUCKING

Around days four, five, and six students are required to complete unknown distance running and rucking events. These will be repeating events of increasing difficulty throughout the remainder of the SFAS. No student can wear a watch. No one knows how long it will continue. No one can safely pace it. Much of it is in sand. You just have to have the stamina required, when required, and to the level required. Throughout Special Forces training you must learn to control fear of the unknown.

FORTY-FIVE POUNDS OR YOU'RE OUT!

The rucking events require that students carry a minimum of 45 pounds not counting weapon or water. There are seven or eight scales in the Camp Mackall barracks area at which students periodically and sometimes randomly are required to throw their rucksack on the scale. If it doesn't weigh 45 pounds or more, you are terminated from the course immediately. Said one student, "You never take a chance. Some of those scales are off and where one might register 47 pounds another might register 42 pounds on the same ruck. When your ruck is placed on the scale there are no allowances for scale calibration. If you are underweight, your ID number is calibrated out the door."

LAND NAVIGATION

Week one also includes classroom land navigation. "Anyone showing up at SFAS without a basic understanding of grid squares, azimuths, back azimuths, true north, grid north, saddles, draws, elevation marks, etc., is going to be at a distinct disadvantage," notes one student. The tempo of training picks up and the opportunities for self-study are very limited. As you will see in subsequent days, it is not just the day and night cross-country navigation that is the real challenge, it is the navigating environment that seriously screws with textbook concepts.

SF students stretch out before the morning ruck march. Day after day the training gets progressively tougher. As time goes on the students will be evaluated on how they are able to resolve complex problems after complete physical and mental fatigue. They are intentionally pushed to the edge of human endurance. The Special Warfare Training Center has studied the science and limits of human endurance. This training will push the envelope. © Hans Halberstadt

A Special Forces NCO leaps blindfolded into the pool as part of the Special Forces water survival test. All students in SFAS will be evaluated for their swim capabilities. For SFAS students, this is an "evaluation" and not yet a "test." Although it is not essential to pass at this point, it is required before you can graduate from the course. Remedial swim training is provided during the course for those who exhibit minor weaknesses, but improving swim skills before entering the Q course is a good idea.

A rope maze confronts this SF student as he claws his way over the top. During the 2-mile run through these obstacles students will become spread out and isolated. Regardless, other students cannot assist or offer verbal encouragement. Future Green Berets are being tested to determine the level of sweat and sinew they can draw from within themselves. © Hans Halberstadt

WEEK TWO
CRAWLING IS OVER . . . START WALKING

The course is becoming more physical now: less classroom time, less sleep, more pain, more challenges to your endurance. Land navigation has moved from inside to outside. You get walking and running pace counts. That is, you determine how many of your steps equal 100, 200, or 300 meters. You learn techniques to counteract "drift" while you track a magnetic azimuth for several kilometers. If you talk to another student searching for his waypoint during land navigation, your next waypoint is the airport ticket office home.

RIFLE PT AND LOG DRILLS

The rifle PT consists of all kinds of gyrations with a weapon held overhead, passed between hands, arms out, and so on. Eventually, you will compete with another student until your arms quiver and drop. Without a break you'll be launched into log drills in the sand pit. Ten students move a massive telephone pole over their right shoulders, their left shoulders, their right shoulders. Screw it up and you are in the sand rolling right and rolling left. Probably the best part of this misery is that you get the rare opportunity to know you are screwing up. During log drills the cadre is known to elevate their

Students are required to carry fellow students or a sand bag with the equivalent weight. This may be unexpectedly integrated at any point during training. The sand-filled bag, called the "sandman," represents a downed pilot. In this photo, a student is in early phases of training since he is carrying no equipment of his own. Later he may have to do the same thing in the middle of a mission with his rifle and gear. © Hans Halberstadt

decibel levels to something akin to the warm and fuzzy sound of a drill sergeant. What a relief!

NASTY NICK

You are now getting an introduction to the grueling descriptions of *Nasty Nick*. You get to see films of him. You get to look at pictures of him. You hear explanations of him. You are provided with advice on how to beat him. You receive instruction on techniques that must be used when you encounter him. The stories about him abound. Can he really be as bad as the images suggest? They are not going to give you a "hands-on" preview. Nasty Nick is a series of 26 contraptions invented by the devil himself and are misleadingly given the benign name of *obstacles*. It is every evil physical challenge that the mind can conjure up over a trek of about 2 miles. The course must

have been designed by aliens who wanted to humble the human race. It will humble you.

The real beauty of preparing for Nasty Nick is that the student must draw on his imagination, attention to detail, retention, visualization, and ability to mentally "act as if" he is negotiating the obstacle without the benefit of actually negotiating it. This is a supremely important skill set in the development of Green Berets. Special Forces soldiers will often face missions where the only practice they will get will be studying the available intelligence in their mind.

The unknown distance runs and rucks continue. A student tells it like this: "They get longer . . . or at least they sure seem longer. Perhaps, the log drills and rifle PT are taking their toll. Although we were all in top physical condition when we began SFAS, most of us have lost 10

Unknown distance ruck marches usually come as a morning wake-up call, but they may be ordered at any time of day or night. These 50- to 60-pound rucks wear down the students, but they are *light* compared to fully combat-loaded rucks that Special Forces students will carry during subsequent phases. It's all part of the "crawl, walk, run" training methodology. © *Hans Halberstadt*

Upper body strength is an essential physical requirement to make it through the dozens of obstacles. Developing good rope-climbing techniques is another area for pre-SF training focus. This student tackles one of the rope obstacles in a pre-dawn climb. Yellow smoke spews from a smoke grenade below the climber. © Hans Halberstadt

This SFAS student sports a smile as he learns that he has found all the correct locations during the STAR night navigation final exam. He has successfully completed this demanding trek through swamps, vines, ravines, and mud up to his knees. Although soaked and tired, he is on his way to being "selected" and that certainly warrants a smile.

to 15 pounds. By the end of SFAS, I didn't recognize some of the guys I had started with. They had lost that much weight."

WEEK THREE
IT'S TIME TO RUN

You will go through Nasty Nick this week. Also, you will undertake more unknown distance rucks, a day-and-night land navigation course, and the final "Trek" with a team of 12 to 15 men. The number of teams and sizes of the teams will depend on how many students still remain in the course. You have probably lost 100 fellow students by now and another 50 will disappear over the next couple of days.

NASTY NICK

A muscular student comments: "I consider myself an excellent rope climber. During some nonevaluated time, a couple of students asked me to show them some rope-climbing techniques. There was a nearby area where I could do a limited demonstration. This was a day or two before we were going to meet Nasty Nick. I started to climb. My arms quivered, and I was forced after just a foot or two to let go. The muscles in my forearms were so stretched and burned out from the log drills that I didn't have the ability to climb 3 feet. When I finally confronted the obstacle course, the adrenaline rush and sheer desire got me through them. There are so many obstacles that I almost missed a few. It's not like there is a whole bunch of students in front of you to follow. At times you feel very much alone."

HURL YOUR BODY

By now the day and night navigation courses have gotten incredibly tough. Not only are the distances to each waypoint further, the terrain is some of the worst you will ever see. At times you have to hurl your body

The obstacle course has nearly 2 miles of obstacles. Students study drawings of each obstacle and mentally rehearse how they will tackle each of them, but they are not allowed to practice or even visually see the actual obstacle. Their first introduction to the obstacle course will be an evaluated training event. This type of mental imaging is a critical skill required of Special Forces soldiers. © Hans Halberstadt

into thorn bushes over and over again just to move several feet. The night navigation sometimes runs into the early morning hours and no one can rest until all of the students have been accounted for. So, if it takes till 4 a.m. to find some lost student, you might only get a few hours sleep before you are back out on runs, ruck marches, and daytime navigation.

STAR

The final land navigation test is completed on terrain that is called the Star. You must accurately find four points on a single day or you must find a total of eight points over three days. These days are referred to as Star 1, Star 2, and Star 3. This is where it really pays to know land navigation inside and out. If you can accurately locate four points on the first day, you are good to go and do not have to continue to Star 2 and Star 3. Those who have to continue through Star 2 and Star 3 resemble the walking dead when they finish.

THE FINAL TREK

You are finally organized as a team. Your team of 12 or so men will navigate over several segments of 10 to 15 kilometers each. The Trek begins on Friday morning and wraps up on Sunday. Once again, the terrain will be devastating. At the end of each segment, your team will encounter a challenge. It might be a downed pilot (in the form of a 200- to 250-pound sand-filled duffle bag). Each team member takes turns carrying the pilot, known as the sandman. Other challenges might be carrying a telephone pole for miles or running backwards for half an hour.

WEEK FOUR

This is a short week. Graduation is Wednesday, but there are still hurdles. During your first week you took a battery of psychological exams. One student describes the questions as being like, "Which do you like better,

flowers or clouds?" or "Which would you rather be, an undertaker or an embalmer?" You think to yourself, Gee, I didn't know there was a difference. A psychologist might interview you and continue with that line of questioning. Your test results, combined with your observed behavior, could be cause for dismissal. And finally, some students are "peered out."

PEERED OUT

Over the period of the last three weeks your fellow students have also observed your behavior and performance. They too must consider whether or not you would pose a risk to the accomplishment of a Special Forces mission. Through an anonymous system, your number might be submitted by a student with a recommendation to eliminate you. If your number happens to appear consistently and it happens to be in keeping with cadre observations, you are history.

While students are not encouraged to "peer out" another student, they do have a responsibility to the integrity of the Green Berets and the lives of their fellow soldiers to point out someone who has consistently demonstrated poor judgment or failed to put in a serious effort. At this point, everyone has been through hell and no student would frivolously make a "peer out" recommendation.

As SFAS winds down, you are among the fortunate few selected to continue in the Special Forces Qualification Course. You are guaranteed a slot (school seat) in Phase II. It will be several months or in some cases, more than a year before many complete other prerequisite training programs required to continue on to Phase II. But the men "selected" on this day have a sense that nothing, no amount of time, no obstacle, no human being, will ever stand in the way of continuing through the rest of the course. Prior to this day, wearing the Green Beret and Special Forces tab was a deep desire; today, it is the most important goal in your life.

A student prepares for a high-altitude jump at the Army Military Free Fall school in Yuma, Arizona. SF students will train to make both high-altitude, low-opening and high-altitude, high-opening jumps, often with oxygen tanks. © Hans Halberstadt

FOUR

This SF soldier has emplaced his M60 machine gun in preparation for attack. The barrel can heat up during a firefight and must be routinely changed or it will become red hot and melt. Also, overheating can cause a "cook-off" where the gun will not stop firing even after releasing the trigger. To counteract a cook-off, the gunner will twist the ammo belt. Machine gunners and their assistants carry extra barrels on a mission. The barrel change out is a simple twist and turn, but in the middle of a firefight timing is everything! © Hans Halberstadt

Phase II: Small Unit Tactics

For some SF students it will have been as much as a year since they finished Phase I. Students selected at the close of Phase I and prior to beginning Phase II are required to have completed Airborne School (if they hadn't previously), and, depending on whether they are officers or enlisted men, their appropriate Army Common Leadership Training (ACLT).

On completion of Phase I, the Special Warfare Center (SWC) has determined and informed you of your Special Forces Military Occupational Specialty (MOS). They did this based on your aptitude testing, previous training, performance during Phase I, and most important, the worldwide requirements of the Special Forces Groups. You have had some time to think about your Special Forces specialty training and you can now calculate about how long it will take you to complete all of the SFQC phases.

The break between Phase I (Selection) and Phase II (Small Unit Tactics) was a painful wait. You are determined that you will not go home until you are wearing a Green Beret and the Special Forces tab. Depending on your MOS that may still be more than a year away. Now the tactical training shifts into high gear.

Phase II, Small Unit Tactics, is often referred to as the Common Skills Phase, because upon completion everyone will have attained a common skill level of training in small unit tactics. This levels the playing field regardless of what previous military training a student has had. Prior-service infantry personnel and students who have previously been through Ranger School play a key role in mentoring other students. The SWC likes to have a good blend of background and experience during this phase. Phase II consists of about a month and a half of honing marksmanship, practicing field craft, conducting reconnaissance, raids, ambushes, patrols, and studying light infantry tactics. You will have live-fire exercises and platoon movement to contact. And the never-ending land-navigation training.

CARDINAL RULE:
YOU CAN NEVER *NOT* KNOW WHERE YOU ARE

"I know how to read a map!" But you can never know how to read a map too well. As one Special Forces soldier tells in a hypothetical story, "Imagine you are on a night patrol, traveling over miles and miles of dense jungle. There are no terrain features, just thick, sticky, wet, unforgiving brush and swamps. The enemy strikes. They have overwhelming force. Your chances of living are slim to none. Your one hope hinges on calling in close air support. Five-hundred-pound bombs, accurately delivered, will *make your day.*"

He continues, "The Air Force forward air controller [FAC] cannot identify your position through the triple-canopy jungle. You must provide accurate grid coordinates of the enemy location and your location. The enemy is now within 100 meters of your position and closing. When you provide grid coordinates to the pilot, you don't even want to think about the consequences to your team if you are off by as much as one digit. This is not the moment you ask yourself, Did we travel 700 meters or 750 meters?" If you are unable to provide timely and accurate information as to your location and the enemy location, the technology of our vast arsenal is rendered impotent. Accurate map reading and the skill to always know *exactly* where you are on a map is often the difference between life and death. It is no small wonder that increasingly difficult land navigation is incorporated into every phase of the Special Forces Qualification Course.

Phase III, Small Unit Training, is focused on conventional tactics and operations such as patrols, ambushes, squad, and platoon movements. The students here have arrived at a rally point (RP) and review their plan of attack based on changing circumstances. Note that even in this hasty meeting, they have posted security. Look closely in the background and you will notice the sentry with his back to the group keeping sharp eyes on the surroundings.
© Hans Halberstadt

A "Rubber Duck," properly called a Zodiac, is being hauled to the water by a group of students. Zodiacs are very useful for Special Ops missions because they can be transported easily, deflated, and hidden. They also traverse rough and shallow water very well. Most important, they are compartmentalized so if a bullet blows a hole in one section the other sections will keep the vessel afloat.
© Hans Halberstadt

A Special Forces team moves silently through a marsh on river operations training. In addition to using these boats on inland waterways, SF also trains to push these watercraft out the back of an airplane over the ocean. The team then parachutes out and subsequently swims to the boat.
Photo © Fred Pushies

SHOOT, MOVE, AND COMMUNICATE

Students concentrate on improving basic combat skills. As one student puts it, "It doesn't matter how much firepower you put out if you are not hitting the enemy." Learning how to *shoot* accurately is one thing, but learning how to shoot accurately under conditions of stress, noise, explosions, confusion, and fear with wounded men and bullets zinging all around you is a truly critical skill. Special Forces students are taught to develop the sense of confidence and maturity that will cause them to rise to the occasion under the worst combat conditions.

Throughout a battle, whether in the offense or defense, *mobility* is essential to survival. There will be times when you cannot communicate with your own elements in combat. Retaining mobility through hasty

evaluations and instinctive responses developed through Tactical Standard Operating Procedures (TSOP) will often win the day. When you lose the flexibility to move you can neither close with the enemy nor escape his withering fire. If you cannot retain mobility, mercy is your improbable alternative.

Finally, effective *communication* during a battle can provide you the opportunity to mass forces and firepower that give you the advantage to checkmate your foe or escape the pending onslaught. Over and over again, students are confronted with situations that require cool-headed, intricate, complex communications during chaos. The age old guidewords; *shoot, move,* and *communicate* are the pillars of an effective combatant. Special Forces students cannot merely be aware of these principles, they must practice them. They must master them.

FIVE-PARAGRAPH FIELD ORDERS

The military teaches a uniform organizational concept for issuing orders that ensures the completeness of the directive. This concept is manifested in the five-paragraph field order. Throughout the Q course, and especially in this phase, you will be required to write and issue five-paragraph orders. In later phases you will have to train others to properly construct and issue these orders. The five paragraphs may include a number of subparagraphs.

This field order process is a method of organizing thoughts, information, and concepts that will cover the primary subjects essential in the planning of tactical military operations. As one student commented, "The five-paragraph field order is just a method of making sure that you covered all your bases." The omission of any given paragraph can gravely impact the outcome of a battle. You are going to have to master the concept in order to graduate.

How extensive the order is will often depend on the level of command. For example: Under paragraph one, Situation, you will always, at a bare minimum, identify the enemy situation, the friendly situation, and the weather and terrain you are facing. As is common throughout the military there are many acronyms developed to help a student recall specifics. One acronym, frequently employed in the development of the Situation portion of the operations order, is called OCOKA (See sidebar).

FIVE-PARAGRAPH FIELD ORDER

1. Situation
2. Mission
3. Execution
4. Service and support
5. Command and signal

OCOKA

Obstacles
Cover and concealment
Observation and fields of fire
Key terrain
Avenues of approach

An SF student demonstrates proper techniques for clearing rooms and buildings in a mock city at Fort Bragg, North Carolina. MOUT (Military Operations in Urban Terrain) is an ever-expanding training piece at the Special Warfare Training Center. SF students will learn how to approach, clear, and secure the cleared area as they proceed through a city-like environment. As one instructor comments, "Preparing SF students to fight in cities is as important today as it was to prepare them to fight in jungles during the Vietnam era." One training piece has not been exchanged for the other. MOUT is merely the addition of another SF combat skill they develop.

IT MAY NOT BE WAR, BUT IT SURE AS HELL AIN'T PEACE

This is how an Army general described the urban combat they encountered in the streets of Somalia. One of the most significant changes SFQC has undergone in recent years is the expansion of urban combat training. Military Operations in Urban Terrain (MOUT) is now a significant training piece. Student training involves how to secure a perimeter, how to approach a building, how to enter a building, how to clear a room, target identification, how to maintain and extend security.

THE KILLING ZONE

You will train at how to set up ambushes and how to create a devastating kill zone. An effective ambush must be a violent event, but many ambushers open up with a massive volume of fire with every soldier firing on fully automatic. This inevitably leads to the entire ambush unit running out of ammunition about the same time. The lull in firing permits your enemy an opportunity to regroup and attack into your position. To prevent this you learn to stagger the men who are on full auto and those who will fire on semi-auto, so that there is a constant volume of fire and little opportunity for the enemy to regroup.

Of course, you would always prefer to be the *ambusher* rather than the *ambushee*, but you need to learn how to respond to the shock of being ambushed. Do you break contact by rapidly leapfrogging backwards, with each man covering the next? If you are in the "kill zone," do you lay low, return fire, and wait for your patrol elements not in the kill zone to flank the ambushers? Do you charge into the ambushers' position as rapidly as possible?

These two students are rehearsing small-unit movement techniques. They are clearly not on an actual training exercise because they have not "painted" (camouflaged) their exposed skin, and their uniforms are entirely too nice. The student on the right is carrying a PRC 77 radio and the antenna is curved horizontally, parallel to the ground to reduce visibility. © Hans Halberstadt

As a patrol moves silently through the woods, every move of the group is either a previously rehearsed drill or developing action directed by arm and hand signals. Verbal commands are minimal if not completely absent. Silent movement techniques are critical to the patrol's survival and accomplishment of their mission. The weapon he is carrying is a Winchester, Model 1200, 12-gauge, pump action shotgun. © Hans Halberstadt

You will learn techniques like stacking a few tracers among the first several rounds you load into your magazine. That way, when you're fighting, you will have a moment or two of advance warning before running out of ammo. The difference between life and death can often be determined by how rapidly you are able to reload. A second or two of advance warning can give you a significant advantage.

FIRE AND MANEUVER AND FIRE AND MOVEMENT

Although these basic infantry concepts are taught in other military courses, in the Q course they are rehearsed to perfection. Fire and movement refers to the alternating movement of individuals being covered by the fire of other individuals. This is often accomplished in pairs or small fire teams of several soldiers. Fire and maneuver refers to, for example, one group of soldiers laying down a base of fire while another complete element sweeps around the flanks. This requires a sufficient volume of suppressive fire so that the enemy is not aware of or is unable to respond to the pending envelopment.

ARTILLERY AND CLOSE AIR SUPPORT

You will be taught how to call in artillery on the enemy position, how to adjust the artillery, and when to initiate a fire for effect (FFE). An FFE is employed when you are absolutely certain you can place fire precisely on the enemy center of mass, and you want maximum punishment on the enemy position. An FFE order causes all supporting artillery to focus their gun tubes on the same basic location and render continuous fire onto that spot. A student who has experienced combat remarks, "I called in a *fire for effect*. I knew that nothing would survive in the grid-square plot that was several hundred meters directly in front of us. This was very heavy artillery being fired from our rear. Rounds came over our heads and struck their targets to our front. The earth trembled and sound was deafening. It is a moving experience when you hear the whirl and whiz of those huge artillery rounds coming in directly over you."

COVER AND CONCEALMENT

"If the enemy can't see you, he can't kill you," says one of the SNCO cadre. The importance of understanding the principles of good cover and concealment is stressed throughout the phase. Cover and concealment has been a serious training consideration since before the time of Roman legionaries, but it has taken on new significance with the advent of thermal imaging and light-intensifying technologies. We can no longer assume that we are the only privileged military forces to possess such equipment. As a Q-course student, you will be taught how to reduce or eliminate your *thermal signature* and how to eliminate the effectiveness of *light-intensifying* technology. These techniques are critical to survival on the modern battlefield.

PLATOON, SQUAD, AND PATROL FORMATIONS

You will practice movement techniques and employ formations based on the acronym, METT-T (Movement, Enemy, Terrain, Troops, and Time available). Your selection of formation must incorporate control, security, and flexibility.

PATROLLING

One of the cadre explains, "A patrol is not a gaggle of men walking quietly down a trail. There are assault elements, security elements, support elements, breeching teams, demolitions teams, and search teams that might be a component of a patrol. Each element has a highly specific role to play and you need to know how to employ them." A reconnaissance patrol, for example, may have both a recon and security element.

A student relates, "In the black of night I could barely see the outline of the man in front of me. We had to keep about a 5-meter separation. When I tried to focus on the student ahead of me I often lost my visual purple. I had to remember to keep my eyes scanning and not concentrate on a single point. One time when we passed up the count, we discovered we were about 10 men short. Not good if we had gotten to our objective and learned that we had lost half our patrol miles back." While approaching the objective, every move is made with incredible stealth. There is no talking, just arm and hand signals. Movement techniques are stressed.

BATTLE DRILLS

Small units engaging in combat operations will encounter many situations where communication is not practical. Squad-size patrols rehearse their battle drills over and over. These are developed as Tactical Standard Operating Procedures (TSOP). It cannot be understated that the importance of instantaneous, reflexive responses to a variety of potential combat scenarios is often the difference between life and death.

This AC-130 Gunship is one of many weapons systems that SF soldiers must learn to employ in a close air support role. The airplane is equipped with a 25mm Gatling gun, a 40mm grenade launcher, and 105mm cannon. It rains death from the sky. When the 25mm rotating Gatling gun is fired at night, it has the appearance of a jagged streak of lightning descending from the sky. There can be no room for map reading or target identification errors when it lets loose its lethal arsenal. Different versions of this aircraft are called "Spooky" or "Spectre."

A Special Forces soldier checks the AK47 weapon of an Afghan Army trainee. Foreign Internal Defense (FID) is one of the five primary Special Forces missions. That is, training foreign soldiers in basic marksmanship, conventional tactics, and battle drills. Phase II of the Q course has two primary objectives: first, to ensure that future SF soldiers become experts in conventional tactics, and second, to develop a level of expertise sufficient to teach foreign soldiers these skills.

Under the guidance of a Special Forces team, a laser beam from an attack fighter aircraft in Afghanistan "lases" the target. This will precede by mere seconds, a 10,000-pound bomb striking. SF students must learn how to employ close air support aircraft using grid coordinates, lasers, and global positioning systems. On the ground, the SF team often "paints" the target with its own laser first. The aircraft then turns on its laser and "locks on" to the ODA's laser beam. The ground-based laser is called a laser target designator (LTD).

An SF soldier training on a Foreign Internal Defense (FID) mission is teaching land navigation techniques. In the absence of a protractor, after determining the correct azimuth, the Army's standard issue compass can be laid on the map to draw out intersections and plot direction. © Fred Pushies

SF students "fast rope" from a CH-47 helicopter. This is a commonly used method of infiltration and extraction where landing is not practical. The CH-47 is a heavy lift and troop transport helicopter that is used throughout the Army. Special Forces, however, uses advanced versions of these aircraft such as the newly produced CH-47G. These are flown by the Army's Special Operations Aviation unit known as the "Night Stalkers." © Fred Pushies

Students are taught to navigate with handheld global positioning systems (GPS) like this Magellan GPS 1000. By no means does this replace the compass, map, and pace count methods of traversing the land. A paradox of Special Forces units is that on one hand they have an abundance of the most high-speed gear ever invented and at the same time they train to function with the most primitive, minimal, and basic equipment. SF training discourages overreliance on modern technology. © Hans Halberstadt

AREA, ZONE, AND ROUTE RECONNAISSANCE

Throughout the training exercises of Phase II, students are pitted against students. This means that students are not facing an enemy force that just got stuck with the extra duty to play the role of opposition force. Your enemy is trying his absolute best to defeat you. As a fellow SF student he is probably going to be pretty darn good at it. So you may be on an area or zone recon to look for enemy activity while the enemy is already on a mission to look for you. Both sides will get intelligence information from local sources. This information is often contradictory.

EVALUATING INTELLIGENCE

An SF officer explains it this way: "There are two critical components to every piece of intelligence: first, the reliability of the source and, second, the probability of the event." He continues, "Say for example that I rate *sources* A through E and I rate *probabilities* 1 through 5. Now, an A1 intelligence report means that this is a *very reliable source* and a *highly probable* event. Imagine the other combinations like an E1 or an A5. In the latter case, we have a very reliable source, but he is telling us a highly unlikely story. We have no reason to believe that some peasant has a 100-megaton nuclear bomb in his horse-drawn wagon." Students going through the Q course will often be provided C3-type information and just what decisions they make based on C3 are evaluated by the cadre. Interpretive skills and efforts to confirm or validate intelligence are critical.

RAPPELLING

You will be trained to rappel from a 40-foot tower as well as from helicopters. You will learn how to make

Rappelling is a basic Special Forces skill. Students will learn how to use various rappelling gear such as ropes, lanyards, harnesses, D-rings, and carabiners. More important, they will learn how to rappel when fancy equipment is not available and construct their own seat harnesses from rope. The rope harness is called a "Swiss seat." © *Hans Halberstadt*

your own "Swiss seat" from rope and carabiners. One student comments, "There is an entirely different sensation when rappelling down a tower or cliff face as compared to dropping out of a chopper. On the tower or cliff, you have the wall or rock to bounce off. In the chopper drop, it seems like we either let out too much rope too fast and have a meeting engagement with the ground, or we are too tenuous and creep down the rope." Neither is acceptable. SF students can expect to frequently employ rappelling techniques as an infiltration method. It is critical that they demonstrate confidence and proficiency.

A student recalls, "On my first tower rappel, I flipped upside down. After some struggle to acquire a good body position, I still had trouble trusting my brake hand. The tendency is to use the lead [guide] hand above your head to break or slow your fall. That is completely wrong! Like everything else, you need to trust the SF cadre and overcome your natural inclinations."

Small unit tactics are based on four elements of combat power: maneuver, firepower, protection, and leadership. The training students receive during this phase is critical to the Special Forces Foreign Internal Defense Mission. Once again, it is not good enough for SF students merely to know how to execute these missions; they must also know how to teach foreign soldiers how to execute. (See the accompanying piece "Missions of the U.S. Army Special Forces.")

MISSIONS OF U.S. ARMY SPECIAL FORCES

Direct Action: This mission includes raids on bridges, dams, enemy airfields, enemy headquarters, power plants, production facilities, shipyards, missile sites, communication facilities, or enemy personnel to seize, capture, or destroy.

Special Reconnaissance. Observing and recording activity, often deep in enemy territory, of significant tactical or strategic value.

Foreign Internal Defense: On the request of governments of allied nations, advise and conduct training for the host government's armed forces on military equipment, organization, and tactics.

Unconventional Warfare: Organizing, training, and guiding local resistance fighters in the overthrow of occupational or corrupt governments.

Counterterrorism: Offensive measures to prevent, deter, preempt, and respond to terrorism. This includes covert missions in hostile, denied, or politically sensitive environments.

In addition to the above missions, SF units conduct counterinsurgency, counter-proliferation of weapons of mass destruction (WMD), psyops, civil affairs, coalition support, combat search-and-rescue and de-mining operations, humanitarian assistance, counter drug, information operations, and many other "special actions."

FIVE

A Special Forces weapons sergeant trains an Afghan Security Forces soldier to fire a 75mm recoilless rifle atop a ridgeline, 1,500 feet above the Pesh Valley, Afghanistan. Special Forces soldiers assigned to Combined Joint Special Operations Task Force–Afghanistan are helping train Afghans to fight terrorists in their own country.

Phase III: Military Occupational Skill (MOS) Training

Just after graduation from SFAS, students are informed of which Military Occupational Specialty (MOS) they will be pursuing in Phase III of the Q course, and for that matter, the rest of their Special Forces career. This assignment may or may not reflect the student's first choice or even the student's previous military specialty. A number of factors, such as the worldwide needs of the Special Forces groups and the student's aptitude as reflected through testing during SFAS, are considered when assigning a soldier's Special Forces primary skill area.

All officers are assigned to the officer training program known as 18-Alpha, which provides instruction on leadership challenges inherent to commanding an operational detachment alpha (ODA). Enlisted personnel may be assigned as a weapons sergeant (18-Bravo), an engineer sergeant (18-Charlie), a medical sergeant (18-Delta), or a communications sergeant (18-Echo). As a Special Forces student, the training you will receive in these areas far exceeds the standards, complexity, and depth found in similar specialties throughout the U.S. Armed Forces. Initial training to develop these individual skills at the level required by Special Forces will range from 65 days to 322 days.

18A: SF OFFICERS' TRAINING

Effectively, commanding any military unit requires more than rank and position. Nowhere is this more true than command of a Special Forces ODA. The degree of mutual dependence among team members requires that the team commander exhibit individual skills and a level of leadership that earns the respect of the entire team. Earning the respect of highly trained and expertly skilled professionals is no easy feat.

EVERY MEMBER
MUST BRING SOMETHING TO THE TABLE

Other than the fact that someone is designated the "leader," what unique skill does the ODA commander bring to the table? In the case of the enlisted men on the team, skill sets are more clearly identifiable. So, theoretically, the medical NCO or the communications sergeant, or the engineer sergeant could double as the team leader. Surely, any member of the team could take command and the team would still function well. But without a trained ODA commander the team would experience a serious deficit. The 18-Alpha program ensures that commissioned officers provide depth and leadership to their outstanding subordinates.

Prior to beginning Phase II, each student officer has to complete the infantry or armor Officer's Advance Course (nine months). The course concentrates on leadership and unit tactics. Most Advance Course graduates will go on to command regular military units with hundreds of men. On completion of training, the Special Forces student will be commanding just 12—but 12 very unique—human beings. During the 18A phase of SFQC, officers study the nuances of their team structure. They learn how to split the team when necessary to accomplish a mission. They are exposed to combat decision-making training that will replicate potential real-world possibilities. Due to the very high impact of Special Forces operations, the SF officer students will be challenged with hypothetical scenarios that have strategic national and international implications.

DECISION MAKING
WITH GLOBAL IMPLICATIONS

As one student officer put it, "The ODA commander has got to be able to synthesize information from every team member and every intelligence source, and thoroughly understand his *own* commander's intent. The team leader has got to be able to grasp *all* the implications of his decisions."

Engineer students pay close attention to an "old-timer" explosives expert who is teaching this group how to wire and employ the TNT, fuses, and detonation cord that are arrayed on the table in front of them.
© Hans Halberstadt

The student goes on to describe a fictitious, but not entirely improbable, scenario: "Imagine that an ODA has been training soldiers in some foreign country for many months. The team has befriended and bonded with the men they have trained. The team is a guest of the host country government. One night the team learns that the very men they have trained are planning on overthrowing their own government in a military coup. During the limited time available, the team commander will not be able to secure guidance from their higher headquarters."

It is the ODA commander who will internalize the implications of acting or failing to act and the ultimate impact on United States foreign policy. The burden and responsibility for sound decision making under such circumstances goes way beyond the normal expectations of a United States Army captain. But this officer is a Special Forces officer, and he will be held to a higher standard.

KNOW SOMETHING ABOUT EVERYTHING AND A LOT ABOUT NOTHING

This tongue-in-cheek comment could aptly describe a newly graduated ODA commander. He will listen and learn from his experienced team members and develop his leadership methods over time. But from the get-go, he must know something about every skill set in his team. He has got to know if they have enough skill to execute a given mission. A good commander must never be guilty of overestimating capabilities. As a former SF commanding general, reflecting on a failed mission in Iran, so aptly stated, "We must never again mistake enthusiasm for skill. The ODA detachment commander must be intimately familiar with the strengths and weaknesses of every member of his team. He must constantly develop training that will fill these holes, and he must plan missions that capitalize on the strengths of each member."

During the 18A training phase, officers will study the concept of operation for each of the primary Special Forces missions. Officer students will be tested for their grasp of the Military Decision Making Process (MDMP), and they will experience what is called the "Meadows Vacation," which is a classified training operation with both urban and rural scenarios.

Another "value-added" service that the detachment commander brings to the ODA is his prior service leadership experiences with conventional military units.

His grasp of armor operations, artillery units, or enemy division-level tactics has numerous implications in Special Forces missions. For example, the fact that an officer may have studied the technical characteristics of long-range Pershing missiles and their launch sequences can play a critical role in an SF team's direct-action mission to terminate enemy missile sites.

As a student officer, SFQC by itself will not make you an expert in each of the primary skill sets, but you will receive more than a rudimentary understanding and proficiency in each team member's skills. The officers' 18A phase training consists of a little more than two months of training on weapons systems, demolitions, medical techniques, and communications equipment and methods. Additionally, you will receive training in primary Special Forces missions such as special reconnaissance, direct action, foreign internal defense, unconventional warfare, and counterterrorism.

SF WEAPONS SERGEANT (18B) MADE IN AMERICA . . . I DON'T THINK SO

It is as important for a Special Forces soldier to know how enemy weapons function as it is to know how U.S. weapons function. Special Forces teams frequently work deep behind enemy lines. They might not be resupplied for many months, or even years. Captured enemy equipment will have more utility to them than American weapons. It might be difficult to acquire American ammunition behind enemy lines. In some instances, ODAs will actually deploy into combat with foreign weapons and leave much of their U.S.-made equipment at home.

The 18B student will get several months' training focused on U.S.- and foreign-made small arms—rifles, pistols, machine guns, submachine guns, anti-tank weapons, air-defense systems, pursuit-denial munitions, crew-served weapons, and mortars. He must also be the expert in calling in direct fire, indirect fire, and close air support. In addition, the SF weapons sergeant is the primary small-unit tactics instructor. It is not uncommon to see 18B students who have previously been through Ranger School, and many will complete Sniper School either before or after the Q course.

There are several methods of calling in close air support. You can use a laser target designator (LTD), global positioning systems (GPS), standard grid coordinates, and sometimes, the least desirable, just marking your flanks and telling the forward air controller (FAC) approximately where the enemy is located in relation to those markers. Regardless of the method, night close air support can be very scary. You hear the jets roaring toward you, but you can see nothing. A moment later they will be "pickling" their bombs. If you have never heard and felt a 500-pound bomb exploding in the same grid square you are in, you are in for a real rude awakening.

A veteran 18B tells a close air support story: "We were using laser target designators out in the desert. At that time, LTDs were a relatively new concept and the batteries had a terribly short life expectancy. We had radio contact with an inbound F-111B fighter-bomber.

When he was about 12 miles out, he called on the radio, 'lase on.' That was our cue to turn the LTD beam onto the target. We focused on the target. The pilot released the laser-guided bomb. It seemed like it was taking forever for the bomb to get to the target. Suddenly we noticed the battery failing and our beam was growing weaker and weaker. We all looked at each other. Without a word, we dropped that damn LTD and ran like hell. Later, after a couple of shots and a beer to calm our nerves, everyone had a good laugh."

TRAIN THE TRAINER

Throughout Special Forces training, a student must not only master his craft, he must be able to effectively train others. This is especially true with the SF weapons sergeant. He will instruct on the proper emplacement of mortars, how to use a plotting board, and how to run the fire direction center. He will train not only his teammates on how to use various foreign weapons, he might well train foreign armies on maintenance and employment of various weapon systems.

Another Special Forces weapons sergeant shares his experience, "Our team had traveled for days through wretched canyons, ravines, and over mountains. Finally we found the band of tribal resistance fighters that we had come to help. They were about 10 klicks from where we had expected to find them. I guess they slept through a map-reading class. I don't think any two of them had the same weapon or, for that matter, even had weapons that had the ammunition type in common.

"Critical positions at their little outpost were manned with 'water-cooled' .30-caliber machine guns. And here we come with our M16s, M4s, M203s, and high-tech gear for our own men. About the only weapon we had in common was the M1911 .45-caliber pistol. That went over like a lead balloon. When we discussed specific missions, these tribesmen were all too quick to point out that the ODA would probably live through the fight because of our high-tech gear. They, on the other hand, were certain that they would die with their obsolete weapons.

Students in the SF weapons sergeant training program become familiar with a wide range of hand guns, rifles, machine guns, antitank weapons, and surface-to-air missiles. One of these rifles depicted here is the H&K Model 21, 7.62mm, semi-automatic, loaded with a 100-round ammo box. It has an effective range of around 500 meters. © Hans Halberstadt

"We had no credibility until we agreed to leave *our* weapons behind. During our first fire fight I used a Tommy gun, my team sergeant lugged along a BAR, the commo sergeant used a Chinese SKS, another guy had an M1 carbine, and the lucky winners of the 'straw draw' had Russian AKs. We were better prepared to do the movie *Tales of the Gun* than we were ready to fight a well-equipped enemy unit. What the hell, you just gotta suck it up sometimes."

DANGEROUS WEAPONS

As the SF weapons sergeant puts it, "We all know that weapons are dangerous to the person not holding one. But some weapons are dangerous to the person firing it." Many foreign weapons are not manufactured to the tight specifications and standards of U.S.-made weapons. As important as it might be to know how to fire foreign weapons, the 18B will also have to learn how to "make safe" various enemy weapons systems. You will study which parts from one weapon will work in another weapon.

YOUR HEADSPACE AND TIMING IS OFF

When a .50-caliber machine gun is fired it gives a very distinctive, *oomph, oomph, oomph* sound. Sometimes the sound pattern gets kind of funky. If the gun begins to fire erratically, it is often because the "headspace or timing" requires adjustment. A device that looks like a thick "feeler gauge" is used to correct the erratic behavior. SF weapons sergeants don't leave home without one. They are also fond of describing someone's bad behavior as a person whose *headspace and timing needs adjustment.* (See the sidebar on 18B weapons systems.)

SF students in the 18 Bravo, weapons sergeant training program must become intimately familiar with both foreign and domestic weapons. The weapon in the foreground is a Russian-made AK47, and in the background is a German-made MP5K machine pistol. The AK is used by hundreds of foreign countries, and the MP5K is often used by SF in close combat or urban environments. © *Hans Halberstadt*

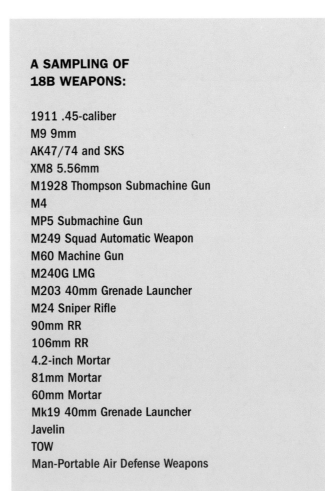

A SAMPLING OF 18B WEAPONS:

1911 .45-caliber
M9 9mm
AK47/74 and SKS
XM8 5.56mm
M1928 Thompson Submachine Gun
M4
MP5 Submachine Gun
M249 Squad Automatic Weapon
M60 Machine Gun
M240G LMG
M203 40mm Grenade Launcher
M24 Sniper Rifle
90mm RR
106mm RR
4.2-inch Mortar
81mm Mortar
60mm Mortar
Mk19 40mm Grenade Launcher
Javelin
TOW
Man-Portable Air Defense Weapons

This is the M57 firing device for a claymore mine. Soldiers refer to it as the "clicker." When the device is depressed it makes a very distinguishing clicking noise. A "click" is often the last sound heard in the life of an approaching enemy soldier. © Hans Halberstadt

A soldier emplaces an M18 Claymore mine. Q course students will use these in both offensive operations, such as ambushes, and defensive operations, such as perimeter security. The mine has a blanket of 700 steel spheres laid over a pound and a half of composite C4. One side clearly states, "This Side Towards Enemy." Enemy forces have been known to creep up in the middle of the night and turn them around. The enemy then makes some noise to entice the defenders to activate the claymore. You may want to consider placing a small piece of reflective tape on the back side. If you don't see the tape, don't activate the mine!

Left: Special Forces engineers will be tasked with providing demolitions training to foreign military personnel in keeping with their SF Foreign Internal Defense (FID) mission. In the photo an SF soldier is training Kuwaiti soldiers on how to employ explosive charges.

Below: A 10th Group Special Forces engineer teaches a Lebanese NCO how to use the Valon 3 metal detector. Special Forces team engineers around the world are involved in de-mining operations. Phase III training for SF students in the 18 Charlie, Special Forces engineer career field will study both U.S. and foreign mines. They must know how to mark, plant, and clear minefields.Of special significance, in recent times, the engineer course teaches SF engineer students how Improvised Explosive Devices (IED) are constructed and defused.

SF ENGINEER SERGEANT (18C)
ARCHITECT, ENGINEER, CONTRACTOR,
DEMOLITIONS EXPERT,
FORTIFICATIONS BUILDER

The 18C team engineer is all of these. Over the two months in this phase, SF engineer students learn to construct bridges, buildings, dams, and fortifications. They also learn how to blow up bridges, buildings, dams, and fortifications. You will work with many different types of explosives as well as electric and nonelectric firing systems. Knowledge to construct facilities has the added benefit of teaching students the critical support characteristics that will be vital to planning sabotage missions.

Students learn how to lay minefields and how to de-mine minefields (counter-mine operations). Training includes how to construct improvised munitions and how to disarm foreign improvised munitions. You will learn how to construct bombs from fuel and other components which, when mixed together, are called *fougasse*. In ancient times fougasse translated as "liquid fire." One day you will read a blueprint and the next day you will calculate the maximum sustainable weight of a bridge or execute a target analysis mission.

The Special Forces engineer must know the critical components in a myriad of strategic facilities, such as hydroelectric plants, power grids, oil refineries, production facilities, coal-fired power plants, missile sites, radar installations, and more. The team engineer must be proficient in both land and water navigation and capable of interpreting maps, overlays, and charts. He will be consulted over and over again as the SF team develops its plans during direct-action missions.

In humanitarian missions and civil action projects the engineer will be the lead team member in designing and constructing water purification systems, buildings, road networks, unimproved airstrips, and defensive fortifications for the community. The 18C construction engineer training covers both wood and masonry construction projects and includes the principles of electrical wiring.

Target analysis is a major function of the SF engineer. "About half my team had gotten to the target area hours ahead of me," relates an SF team engineer. "When I got there, I found the team all taking bets on the best way to blow a hole in the floor of a building that we needed to check out. They were waiting for my expertise and, more important, for me to resolve the winner of this high-stakes game. For the last two hours these guys had speculated on TNT, C-4, building a shape charge, and every imaginable manner to get access to the area below the floor.

"I studied the floor area for a moment, removed my bayonet, and pried it between two of the floor timbers. A 5-foot section of the floor began to crumble. I looked up at a half dozen bewildered, embarrassed, and dumb looks. They *all* lost!" This was evidently a hard lesson in the age-old adage, KISS (Keep It Simple, Stupid).

An SF engineer student focuses intensely on measuring the exact amount of fuse and detonation cord required to build an explosive charge. A great deal of measurements and mathematics goes into analyzing a target and developing the right amount and type of explosives to demolish it. © *Fred Pushies*

SF MEDICAL SERGEANT (18D)
TEAM MOM

In the words of an experienced SF medical sergeant: "The ODA team sergeant is the team *dad*. The medic is the team *mom*." The medical sergeant knows the most personal details of every man of the team. He requires maturity usually found only in very experienced doctors. The team medical sergeant must develop a broad range of skills. He must be a healer, a source of comfort, and yet, like his teammates, he must also be an extraordinary fighter.

The first 24 weeks of the nearly year-long training cycle for SF medics is called the Special Operations Combat Medic (SOCM) course. During SOCM the SF medical student is accompanied by medical students from other branches of the Army and other branches of the Armed Forces. It is not uncommon for fellow students to be Army Rangers, Special Operations Aviation, Special Operations Support Battalion medics, Marine Force Recon, Navy SEALs, or Air Force Para Rescue.

THE STREETS AND BACK ALLEYS

In addition to training focused on anatomy and physiology, SOCM students work in some of the most dangerous streets of major cities in the United States. They function side by side with paramedics and emergency room doctors. They don't just read about "invasive medicine," they physically perform it. SF students execute hands-on procedures that many medical interns are not exposed to for years.

Prior to students working on real patients, they will have performed these invasive procedures on one another. As one student comments, "You really have to keep in mind to be *gentle* on your patient, because just a short while later, you will be your patient's patient."

On successful completion of the SOCM, the American Heart Association certifies the students in Advance Cardiac Life Support (ACLS) and the National Registry of Emergency Medical Technicians certifies the students at the EMT Basic and Paramedic level. On the battlefield these

A Special Forces student tends to a trauma patient simulating possible head and neck injuries. Students often joke that it is wise to remember the golden rule when performing invasive procedures on one another. These are often graded exercises under the watchful eyes of experienced medical professionals. © *Fred Pushies*

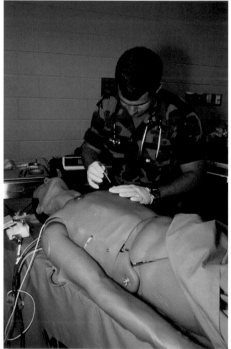

SF medical students have opportunities to practice on dummies before they practice on each other. The "dummies" get more working parts with each new model and quite a lot of good training comes from these simulators. © *Fred Pushies*

medical students will not have an "on-call" doctor. To the extent that circumstances will permit, the hospitals that support this training know that the students need to be exposed to a wide variety of medical emergencies. And they are.

DUCK-BILLED PLATYPUSES

This is how an ODA team medic describes the conundrum of the SF medic: "With one exception, all medical personnel on the battlefield are afforded a unique Geneva Convention status. The exception is the Special Forces medic. Traditional medical personnel do not carry weapons and are not combatants. The SF team medic is both a fighter and a healer. He may shoot an enemy fighter and pull the bullet out of the same man five minutes later." This paradox is a mental challenge unique to the Special Forces medic.

SPINNING BLOOD IN THE BRUSH

Field expedient procedures under the harshest conditions are necessary training components of the SF medical student. In far-flung villages, hamlets, mountains, and jungles, the SF medic does not have the luxury of sending his patient to the hospital's third floor for a blood test and diagnosis. He will spin the

blood, insert catheters, hook up IVs, perform rectal exams, and install nasal-gastric tubes. From the perspective of a wounded Special Forces team member in the mountains of Afghanistan, or the African village chief whose young son is dying of cholera, the SF medic may as well be "the healing angel." Preparing students to shoulder this awesome responsibility is incorporated throughout their training.

Following SOCM, SF students continue on for 22 more weeks of training in the Special Forces Medical Sergeants' (SFMS) course. At Fort Bragg, the most advanced, state-of-the-art, three-dimensional medical software and computer programs are made available for student studies. Additionally, SFMS will include more time in civilian health-care facilities. Their training includes combat trauma, advanced echelons of care, preventative medicine; differential diagnostics; infectious control; nursing; environmental medicine; proper surgery; local, regional, and general anesthesiology; pharmacology; dental; pediatrics; labor and delivery; immunization; invasive and noninvasive procedures; animal husbandry; and improvised medical techniques. The SF medic must know what to do and what to use, even when the medications are labeled in Arabic or Mandarin.

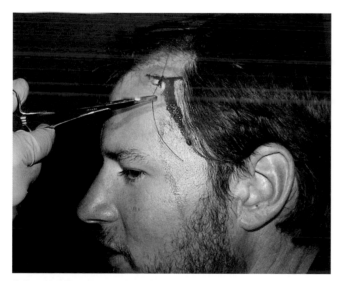

A Special Forces medic stitches up a minor cut. The team medical sergeant will teach this and many other medical skills to all team members. Still, other team members will be understudies to one another since every member is required to develop a secondary skill set.

For the Special Forces medical sergeant, his operating room is often wherever he happens to find the casualty. He rarely has the luxury of a mobile Army hospital anywhere near his location. In this photo, the team medic is fixing up an injured team member on the hood of their Humvee in Afghanistan.

Throughout the SF medical sergeant's training, the emphasis is on medical principles. To quote one of the medical instructors: "If you understand physiology behind what's wrong, and stick to solid medical management principles, you can develop a treatment, even when that treatment seems extremely unconventional." Special Forces soldiers are, after all, "unconventional warriors."

SPECIAL FORCES
COMMUNICATIONS SERGEANT (18E)
MOST PRIMITIVE AND MOST SOPHISTICATED

During the nearly four-month-long SF communications training phase, you will learn how to communicate with the best equipment and you will learn how to communicate with next to nothing. You will learn how to string antennas through the trees and how to use bed springs to construct a radio. You will also be trained on the most advanced communications, encryption, and computer gear in the world.

You will develop understanding of FM, AM, HF, VHF, UHF, and SHF communication systems. A primary method of communications employed by Special Forces is to *burst* their message traffic. The intended message is first developed normally. It is then encoded and compacted electronically. At the specified time the message is transmitted. At the receiving station, it is expanded and decoded. The entire time the message was "in the air" may have been just seconds or even just milliseconds. This greatly reduces the potential for enemy intercept and also prevents the enemy from triangulating the location of the transmission.

When this technique is employed on a submarine, the sub floats the message in a transmitter to the surface. After the sub is safely out of the area, the message "bursts." The transmitter and message then self-destruct and no one is the wiser as to where the sub has gone.

Students gain a thorough understanding of antenna theory and wire communications. Satellite communications gear is used throughout this training. You will employ digital encoding equipment and learn the fundamentals of cryptography. At the same time you will learn how to develop a home-made encryption system when nothing else is available.

Emphasis is placed on field-expedient methods of communicating. Students learn how to deal with sunspots and solar flux. They work on constructing "long wire" antennas as well as employing dipoles and parasitic arrays. You must develop proficiency in Morse code, and quite a bit of your training will focus on foreign communications equipment.

SF communicators are notorious for playing practical jokes on their teams. The technology is increasingly more complex, and some of the bizarre communication methods actually do work. As long as the commo guy can keep a straight face, he can really put one over. An experienced ODA communications sergeant will have dozens of good stories about how he made his team help with setting up antennas. Don't be surprised if he actually convinces his team to climb trees, spread their arms and face north with their heads cocked on a 45-degree angle. But when the chips are down, these same commo guys can create miracles with a few pieces of tin, part of a metal boat, and some wire. SF communications sergeants have been known to make an antenna out of bed springs.

One SFer relates this story: "We had completed our mission and left the country. We were all in our civilian clothes when we arrived back in the U.S., where we checked into a Holiday Inn. One of the team members recalled a critical piece of information that needed to get to the team that had replaced us. Well, it wasn't like we could just pick up the telephone and call them in the middle of the jungle. We knew when the in-country team would be monitoring the radio. So out behind the hotel, we found some trees and constructed an antenna out of wire we picked up at a local hardware store. Two of the guys were up in trees stringing wire, and I was on the ground with the hardware (covered). We got through to the other team, but I often wondered what the hotel maids thought about us."

EYES AND EARS OF THE TEAM

Communications is the lifeblood of a Special Forces team. Entire missions depend on communicating developments in an accurate and timely manner. Whether transmitting vital information to higher headquarters, coordinating resupply, evacuating wounded, or requesting a hasty extraction, your ODA needs to talk to the outside world, and it's the communications sergeant they all depend on. Without "good comms," an ODA is a bunch of highly trained professionals with very limited ability to influence events.

The SCR 100 satellite radio is just one of dozens of radio systems that the SF communications sergeant must know how to operate and maintain. This unit will allow a team to transmit secure communications from anywhere to anywhere on the globe. Radio technology is constantly improving with smaller and more efficient units being produced on the heels of each new version. © Hans Halberstadt

A Special Forces ODA communications sergeant in Afghanistan emplaces his satellite radio antenna in preparation for a scheduled contact with higher headquarters. A narrow window of time is established for each contact. If the team misses the time window the absence of critical nformation might seriously impair their mission. The Special Forces communications training is the second longest course of instruction behind the SF medical training program.

SIX

A resistance fighter, armed with an AK47 and 30-round "banana clip" magazine, is in position for the final assault. If the student ODA fails to plan and advise properly for critical events of the operation, the Gs will make certain that the unplanned segment goes haywire. The ODA will be faced with unexpected problems and challenges as a consequence of poor prior planning. A good plan has "what-if'd" every course of action and every contingency. SF soldiers must be experts in analyzing plans. © Hans Halberstadt

Phase IV: Unconventional Warfare

THE COUNTRY OF PINELAND

You are preparing to infiltrate Pineland. This exercise is called "Robin Sage." For this training, you be will assigned to a 12-man student team, complete with all the appropriate positions found in an ODA. Positions like the team warrant officer or team intelligence NCO will be represented by randomly selected students. The critical position of team sergeant (18Z) will be rotated among the NCO students assigned to the team. You will never know when the cadre might tap you on the shoulder and inform you that you are now the team sergeant.

Throughout every phase of SFQC you have been fed information about the fictitious country known as Pineland. You have known all along that some day you would have to help the residents of Pineland regain their freedom. Whenever time permitted, you studied the country. Expert knowledge of Pineland will be critical to passing Robin Sage, which is the Phase IV culmination exercise. It is also one of most important training aspects of the entire Special Forces Qualification Course.

An SF student in "isolation" is working on mission planning for his team. Before the team is ready to brief the commander, the team will have examined and developed matrixes on hundreds of pieces of information to create the most efficient and executable plan. The plan must be bulletproof.
© Hans Halberstadt

A map reconnaissance of "Pineland" is far more than getting a rough idea of where you are going. Students have to know every last detail of the terrain they will traverse. Elevations, contour lines, draws, ravines, saddles, marshes, and wood lines are all taken into consideration when determining routes of ingress and egress. Much of this information is required knowledge to be demonstrated during each student's segment of the briefback and the Isolation Facts (ISOFAC) exam before deployment. © Hans Halberstadt

Fictitious as it may be, this training exercise into Pineland encompasses thousands of square miles and 12 counties of rural North Carolina. Hundreds of civilians, businesses, and government agencies participate and support this phase of SFQC. Many of them have helped train U.S Army Special Forces soldiers for so long that their fathers and grandfathers participated in Robin Sage nearly 50 years ago.

Pineland is controlled by an oppressive, tyrannical government. Human rights are ignored. Elements of the population have taken up arms against this oppression. These disparate indigenous groups of resistance fighters are hiding in the mountains and forest. Their commonality is that they intensely resent the government of Pineland. Nevertheless, even among the different enclaves of resistance fighters they have intense disagreements and power struggles.

In addition to their common external enemy and their conflicts with other resistance groups, the resistance fighters have internal problems with respect to definitions of roles, responsibilities, equipment, training, and motivation. Their effectiveness as fighters is seriously impaired by these problems. While on one hand they want American support to help overthrow Pineland's government, they differ as to the type and degree of support they want. Some of these fighters have emerging personal agendas that take priority over their dedication to the cause. Student ODAs will be given the mission to fix this situation, overthrow the bad guys, and help the indigenous fighters retake their country and restore democracy.

GUERRILLAS

The resistance fighters ("good guys") are hiding in various locations throughout the wilderness areas. These fighters might be called freedom fighters, resistance fighters, indigenous fighters, or any number of other terms. During Robin Sage they are all called "guerrillas" or "Gs." The top dog in each group is referred to as the G chief. The guerrillas have support from portions of the population that are either actively supporting them or at least sympathetic to their goals. These people are called "auxiliaries." There are hundreds of opposition force soldiers (OPFOR, a.k.a., "bad guys") attempting to hunt down the guerillas.

A Special Forces soldier moves through the jungle with an FN-MAG 58 machine gun. The MAG 58 is a close cousin to the U.S. military's 7.62mm M60 and is used by more than eighty countries. The weapon incorporates features from Browning's tried and true M1918 BAR. The action has been turned upside-down and modified to accept belt feed. Green Berets must become as familiar with foreign weapons as they are with U.S.-made firearms.

INCORPORATING COMBAT EXPERIENCES

The scenarios in Robin Sage are continuously updated to reflect the combat experiences of Special Forces teams fighting in Afghanistan and Iraq. In fact, many of the cadre and Gs have served in those countries and are role players for this exercise. Training doesn't get any more real than this.

A recent Q course officer comments, "Returning officers from Afghanistan always stressed how similar Robin Sage was to their experiences in combat. Interestingly enough, less than a month after receiving my SF tab, I was also in Afghanistan, meeting, eating, and dealing with the local warlords and civic leaders. They were almost carbon copies of my interface with the Gs in Pineland.

SERIOUS BUSINESS

To the uneducated this sounds like a bunch of fun. Do not get lulled into a sense of child's play about this war game. There is no room for antics or cowboys here. You will find that Robin Sage is physically exhausting and mentally challenging. It requires every skill that you have been taught. This training is deadly serious business and students who miss that message will not pass the Q course. Phase IV and its culmination in the Robin Sage exercise is what Special Forces is all about.

Robin Sage closely replicates missions that Special Forces teams around the world have been executing for many years. In fact, SF traces its lineage back to the First Special Service Force (Devil's Brigade) and derives its heritage from the early OSS/Jedburgh teams of World War II. These teams were parachuted into France behind enemy lines with the mission of developing the French Resistance fighters.

At the same time, in other parts of the world, the forefathers of Special Forces were working with natives in the jungles of Burma and launching critical missions deep in the enemy's rear. In Vietnam, Special Forces trained thousands of Montagnard tribesmen to fight on the side of South Vietnam. They became some of the most effective fighters in that war. Special Forces infiltrated Afghanistan and worked with the Northern Alliance to defeat the oppressive Taliban regime. In countless other nations, Special Forces teams have worked on the side of freedom and democracy.

SPECIAL FORCES ARE UNIQUE

Few people understand the differences between Special Forces (SF) and other Special *Operating* Forces (SOF), such as the Navy SEALs or Army Rangers. Robin Sage and the training leading up to it best illustrate these differences. Special Forces must learn all the fighting skills and tactics of elite commando-type soldiers. They must be able to execute a wide range of direct-action and reconnaissance missions. The most notable differences are that SF soldiers must also master the ability to work with a wide variety of foreigners. They must be capable of transferring military skills and organizing foreign fighters into effective military units. Recent images of Special Forces soldiers in Afghanistan, on horseback and fighting alongside the Northern Alliance resistance fighters epitomize these employment differences.

Unlike many commando units that execute a mission and then return to their base, the SF soldier must be prepared for long-term survival without resupply. He must understand the nuances of different religions, cultures, politics, equipment, and medicine. He must be expert in the characteristics of the countries, languages, and of the area in which he will operate. SF soldiers must have the maturity to identify, understand, and respond to their foreign counterparts' idiosyncrasies. The inability to grasp these subtleties could result in mission failure and even death. Robin Sage is designed to test these skills.

ISOLATION

The first part of every Special Forces mission is placing the ODA into "isolation." This is where the teams receive their mission and prepare to deploy into Pineland.

COUNTER-GUERRILLA WARFARE

Inherent in the ability to organize and train guerrillas are the skills necessary to defeat guerillas. Another SF mission. Special Forces have been used to locate Communist guerrillas in South America, such as Che Gueverra, Castro's point man for inciting the Communist overthrow of other governments. In recent years, Special Forces teams were instrumental in defeating insurgents in El Salvador and have assisted the Philippine government in the defeat of insurgents in remote jungles. Many host governments are not anxious to publicize their request for U.S. Special Forces assistance. Many SF counter-insurgency missions remain "classified."

A single ODA is capable of training, advising, assisting, or directing foreign counterparts in their functional areas up through battalion level (FM 3-05.20, Special Forces Operations).

The OPFOR (Opposition Forces, a.k.a., enemy) are often made up of highly skilled troops from the 82nd Airborne Division. After repeated cycles of testing SF students, these OPFOR soldiers are pretty wise to SF operational tactics. Student ODAs will be challenged to come up with truly creative methods if they hope to beat the OPFOR. © Hans Halberstadt

Not all infiltration jumps are out of fixed-wing aircraft. In this photo, the soldiers are conducting a nonequipment training jump from an MH-60 Black Hawk helicopter. There is still a strap running across the front of the jumpers. However, that strap is removed several minutes before exiting. When there is no strap and the chopper banks to align for its final run over the drop zone (DZ), you have a sensation that you are going to simply slide out before getting to the DZ.

Some soldiers will be infiltrated by helicopter or driven in a truck to the edges of Pineland. Those who "jump" in get to avoid a long bumpy ride, but they are very conscious of not wanting to incur an injury during the night jump. An injury would subject the student to be "recycled" back to the beginning of this important phase. Many students would just as soon "ride" this mission into Pineland.

The MC Combat Talon, used often by Army Special Forces and flown by the Air Force Special Operations Wing, is seen here deploying missile countermeasures. This aircraft, although resembling a C-130, is extensively modified with electronics for a low-level map of the earth infiltrations. It is equipped with terrain-following and terrain-avoidance radar and an nertial global-positioning satellite system. It is able to locate smaller drop zones and deliver SF paratroopers with greater accuracy than conventional C-130s.

The team weapons sergeant is a driving force in the training of the indigenous resistance fighters. He is responsible for planning much of the training to include the use of these antitank weapons, marksmanship, light and heavy machine guns, rocket-propelled grenade launchers, and small unit tactics. © Hans Halberstadt

Isolation is accomplished at a location known as the Special Forces Forward Operating Base (SFOB). The SFOB is run by the team's higher headquarters and is normally in a very "high-security" compound surrounded by lots of barbed wire and no-nonsense guards with submachine guns.

The isolation area may as well be a black hole in space, because once an isolation area goes "hot" nothing goes in or comes out of the SFOB without passing extensive, excruciating security checks. Every inch of the SFOB is electronically swept to detect possible bugs (eavesdropping technology). Procedures for communicating with a team in isolation are extremely stringent and they are enforced to the letter. An SFOB is probably as secure as the gold at Fort Knox.

An isolated ODA will have no communication with the "outside world" until the mission is over. On actual missions, dying uncles or childbirth are not causes for communication with an SF soldier in isolation. Here, in a student training environment, some exceptions to the restricted communication procedures will be accomodated if necessary.

Now your ODA will be briefed by the SFOB commander on the pending mission. The SFOB staff of experts will be available to answer general questions about the mission, the country, the enemy, and the friendlies in the operational area. Your ODA will be taking copious notes. Your team will be told how many days it has to prepare a concept of operation and plans to execute the mission. Your ODA will hold in abeyance many specific questions until you begin actual development of a specific plan.

The SFOB commander does not dictate to you how your team is to accomplish the mission. He gives the mission. He gives support. He provides every expert imaginable and nearly every resource the team requests. He may review mission constraints, such as the only type of aircraft available, but constraints are normally few and far between.

No SF commander wants to limit the imagination of the ODA. He depends on the team to demonstrate intelligence, creativity, and ingenuity, and to incorporate efficiency into your planning. In a real mission, it will be *your* lives on the line, so it needs to be *your* plan. This absence of highly specific guidance often results in the ODA generating a unique solution. That's why they call them Special Forces.

YOU WANT WHAT?

As a team develops its plan, it often needs to check on the availability of specific equipment and may even request an opportunity to train on the equipment before mission deployment. Through an elaborate messaging system it requests these items from the SFOB staff. Some truly remarkable requests emerge from isolated teams. How many diesel locomotives did you say you need? You may find the SFOB operations officer or even the SFOB commander asking for an early overview of your plan before he launches Herculean attempts to get your locomotives. If the request makes sense and can be substantiated by a solid executable plan, the SFOB will move mountains in an attempt to accommodate the ODA. The collective energy of the entire FOB staff and the deploying teams defies description. All energy is focused on the success of the ODA mission.

THE BRIEFBACK

This is the moment of truth. Every detail of the mission has been thought out by the team. The SFOB has laid on the air assets, ground transportation, specialized equipment, satellite imagery, high-tech communications, and mission-specific weapons. It might even have inserted additional agents into Pineland, as your ODA requested.

The SFOB has supported your team in nearly every reasonable request. It is the ODA's time to shine. You will pack everything for the mission. In addition to your personal gear and ammunition, the team will divide up other mission-essential equipment. You might parachute in with a hand-crank generator, a 5-gallon can of water, or claymore mines. You will commit every last detail to memory. Your team has rehearsed every back-up plan and the responsibilities of other team members if any member is injured or wanted. You have questioned and requestioned each other. Now it is time to brief the SFOB commander and his staff.

The detachment commander briefs the overall concept of operation and then each team member briefs his responsibilities. Briefbacks are extremely intense. When the SFOB commander enters the room and in the moments before the detachment commander begins to speak, you can cut the thick air with a knife. The team leader is staking his professionalism and even his career on the soundness of the plan. In Special Forces there is little tolerance for a poorly developed plan.

PACE

Committing every aspect of a mission to memory can be a daunting challenge. SF teams use the acronym PACE (Primary, Alternate, Contingency, and Emergency) to develop their four courses of action. When certain triggering indicators are present, team members instinctively execute the components on one of those four mission options. Teams will develop extensive and well-rehearsed standard operating procedures (SOPs) so that the requirements for new facts and procedures can be kept to a minimum.

A student provides this example: PRIMARY link up "here," ALTERNATE 1 kilometer north in one hour, CONTINGENCY 1 kilometer east of alternate in two hours, EMERGENCY 1 kilometer south of CONTINGENCY in three hours. All are based on clockwise movement, one hour apart. All you really have to remember is the first link-up point and time. If you miss the PRIMARY, you can go straight to the CONTINGENCY, and still make the time.

After each team member has been briefed, the detachment commander sums up the concept and usually concludes with, "Sir, ODA 999 is prepared to execute this mission. What are your questions?" Another moment of deafening silence falls on the room. Customarily, the SFOB commander reserves his questions until his staff has had an opportunity to question the intricacies of the team's plan. The SFOB operations officer, the intelligence officer, the logistics officer, the surgeon, and other experts ask questions aimed at determining the soundness of the plan. The engineer might be asked questions about the communications sergeant's responsibilities, and vice versa. Often the volume of questions will be fewer if the plan is well briefed. Everyone asks if the ODA has everything it needs to accomplish its mission.

Finally, it is clear that the staff questions are done. By now, evidence reflecting the team's planning thoroughness,

or lack thereof, will be clear to everyone in the room. Remember that nearly everyone in the room has served on an ODA. They have run hundreds of missions. They have seen failures and success. This is a pretty tough crowd to impress. It would be an understatement to say that the SFOB staff is good at quickly weeding out and exposing weak plans.

Now the SFOB commander poses a few thoughtful questions. Perhaps he wants some seemingly minor detail reviewed again. He might make some suggestions. He might direct a staff member to add a piece of equipment for the team. The third and final long silence falls on the room. The apprehension is almost unbearable. The SFOB commander looks into the eyes of the men who will face untold dangers and says something like, "ODA 999, you are good to go. Good luck!"

How an ODA team maintains professionalism and doesn't yelp with glee at that moment has always baffled me. Of course there are some ODAs that do not get a "Go." For obvious reasons they are called "No Gos." The most fortunate of those will get an opportunity to rewrite its plan. This would suggest that the flaws were relatively minor or that the commander had a rare moment of compassion. For most No Gos, compassion is not in the cards.

The role players for the SFOB commander are usually "real-world" battalion commanders from the SF groups at Fort Bragg. As one student reflects, "It was really nice to get that perspective from someone outside of the schoolhouse and offer insights other than the schoolhouse solution."

ISOFAC

In addition to the SFOB commander's evaluation of the student ODA's briefback, in Robin Sage each student must pass the ISOFAC (Isolation Facts) test. This is an exhaustive exam on the characteristics of the Pineland, the G force, and the team's plan. A failure on ISOFAC can result in the student not infiltrating into Pineland and being denied the opportunity for recycle.

CHUTE UP!

Your team will parachute into Pineland. Some other teams will insert by helicopter or truck. When you're done putting on your ruck and chuting up, you will be loaded down with more than 150 pounds of equipment and your weapon. You now resemble a fat penguin. Movement anywhere is painful. You just look for a spot to collapse while waiting for the airplane. You are so loaded down that getting back up is impossible without a helping hand.

This will be a night jump. You board a C-130 Hercules aircraft from the back ramp. You are packed in like sardines. You can barely move. Lights are dim to preserve your night vision. Sweat is pouring down your camouflaged face, messing up your great artwork. There's not a lot of discussion. Every man's thoughts are on the mission ahead and the pain of the weight he is carrying. At times like this it always seems that you have to go to the bathroom. Banish the thought. It ain't gonna happen.

No one wants to screw this up. Not for himself or his team. The hydraulics pull up the back ramp. The turbo-prop engines pick up tempo. The airplane begins a slow roll. The Special Forces jumpmaster and the Air Force crew chief are talking near the rear door, reviewing some last-minute procedures. You take a deep breath and close your eyes. You ask your God for strength and wisdom. You have come too far to fail now. You exhale. You think to yourself, "Let's get on with it." The plane seems to roll forever down the runway. Finally, in the cockpit, the aircraft commander says "Rotate," and the plane begins to rise. For some reason you sense momentary relief from the constant stress you have felt the last several weeks.

"OUTBOARD PERSONNEL STAND UP!"

The jumpmaster begins the familiar jump-command sequence. The rear doors open. Wind howls through the fuselage. The fresh air is a welcome relief from the odors of aircraft lubricants, insect repellant, and the body heat of 40 combat-equipped jumpers. The lead man is ordered, "Stand in the door!" The equipment weight and difficulty of movement causes you to reflect, "I just can't get out of this plane fast enough. Damn, where's that *green* light?" Later, you will laugh to yourself when thinking of your impatience and remember, in jump school, when the green light nearly terrorized you? How things have changed.

Chute Up: This student has chuted up and is waiting for his flight into Pineland. He has a main parachute on his back, a reserve chute over his belly, his rucksack suspended below the reserve, and his weapon is in a container along his right side. Jumps are sometimes made with an "open" weapon, that is, not in a container. The yellow line over his shoulder is his static line run from his main chute and clipped onto the reserve carrying handle. © *Hans Halberstadt*

YOU *FALL* OUT

In theory you are supposed to execute a vigorous jump—vigorous enough to clear the turbo-prop blast. With all the weight you are carrying your exit is weak. Your body tumbles in the turbulence of the prop blast. You struggle to maintain a tight body position. You hope that your exit was not so weak that you get banged along the side of the airplane. You are okay. Your chute opens. For a moment you experience relief from the strain of the weight. It will be short-lived relief.

You jumped at an altitude of around 1,000 feet AGL (above ground level), so you are on the ground in a little more than a minute. The moment your chute "pops" and you know you have a good canopy, you attempt to get your bearings. As you look down into the black abyss below, for a split second you fear that you are over water. Then you are able to make out some terrain features. You are where you are supposed to be. You know the area is crawling with OPFOR. For all intents and purposes the training leading up to this moment has you so hyped up that a physiologist or neurologist would not discern a difference in this response to training to that of an actual combat mission.

You get a fix on the target landing spot and begin to maneuver your chute toward it. In the darkness, you see the chutes of some of your teammates below and to your flanks. At about 150 feet in the air you release your lowering line, which drops your rucksack about 30 feet below you. A few seconds later (your fall rate is around 20 feet per second) you hear the ruck hit solid ground. You are now "holding into the wind" and impact the ground while executing your instinctive parachute landing fall procedure. No matter how good your technique, it is rarely a pleasant landing. Rocks, thorns, holes, and the like cause you to mumble a few expletives. Tonight, the rough landing is just a nuisance. Your mind is totally preoccupied with the mission.

A student adds this advice: "If your plan outlines burying your jump gear, be careful; the cadre might make you do that. Remember, that's a big hole to dig, at night, with a D-handled shovel, and still make your link-up time. A better plan would be to load up the parachute kit bags with rocks and sink them in the nearest lake."

On an actual mission this method of disposal would be acceptable. In training, although the plan is fine, the instructors will stop you before the equipment actually goes to the lake bottom.

Your team meets up at a rally point and caches the main parachutes, reserve chute, and helmets. You put on patrol caps and begin to move over miles of dense woods, hills, and sinking mud toward the rendezvous with a friendly agent. The agent will guide you toward the Gs that you are in Pineland to support, but you must make it to the link-up point before dawn. If your team misses the link-up time you will have serious problems.

THE FOG OF WAR

Not all teams are infiltrated where they had planned to be. The cadre will often introduce elements of "friction" into the exercise and mistakes happen. How you deal with them is the challenge. Special Forces students are expected to work through the "fog of war" and develop solutions to unplanned and unfolding events.

A student remembers the infiltration night: "My ODA was driven by truck (under tarps in the back; no light, no talking, no looking out to try to plot our course). We barely made it through the checkpoint with fingers on our trigger guards as the guards poked and prodded the tarps. We were unceremoniously dropped off by the side of a road. We had no idea where we were. We missed our contact and spent the night in a cigar-shaped perimeter waiting for our link-up (not according to plan). By dawn, the cadre, finally sick of waiting, read us the riot act and pointed us in the right direction. By then it was light and our movement was much faster and quieter than it would have been at night, so, we still made our contingency link-up on time."

The loads don't get any lighter after SF training. This Special Forces NCO is waiting at the airhead to load out for a full combat-equipment jump. Everything on his person and all the equipment underneath him will go out the aircraft door with him. It is a safe bet that he is lugging well more than 150 pounds into the airplane and out the door. © Hans Halberstadt

107

LINK-UP

Your team makes it to the link-up site ahead of schedule. You take up positions in strategic locations to observe activity surrounding the link-up point. When the agent appears in the site, you look for a *far recognition signal.* You will not expose any team member until the proper signal is rendered. If the agent is identified and the signal is correct, one team member will approach the agent. As he is passing the agent, *a near recognition signal* will be rendered. If the far recognition signal is correct but the near recognition signal is incorrect, it is a sure bet that the real agent was compromised and this is a setup. The team member attempting the near signal is probably going to be a dead man. Perhaps you glean some small sense of comfort from knowing that the phony agent is also going to die when your team takes him or her under fire.

It has rained through the night. You are sopping wet. Most of your face paint now looks like blotches of mud. You haven't slept in almost 24 hours. It is BMNT—before morning nautical twilight. Your team splits into multiple locations to observe the link-up point and, if necessary, to be able to fire on it. At dawn you see a young girl riding horseback on a back country trail. She is coming toward you. This should be the agent. In the damp morning, a million mosquitoes are circling your face. There are so many that they get on your eyelids and spot up your vision as you peer through your binoculars.

The girl stops for a moment to rub the horse's face and then removes her riding cap and tosses her hair. This is the correct far recognition signal. But wait! She seems to be a redhead. When you were in isolation you were told to expect a brunette. Is this a trap? Did the enemy capture the real agent and make her talk? Do you send out the team member to test the near recognition signal? If you don't, how will you ever link up with the G forces? This is the first of many times that the success or failure of your mission will rest on your decision at this moment.

These students are disembarking from their long ride into Pineland. The men in black are their G force guides who will lead them to the resistance fighter's camp. During their infiltration drive across country the SF students encounter checkpoints and searches that they must be prepared to deal with. Don't expect a welcoming committee. The guerrillas (resistance fighters), also known simply as Gs, are not a friendly bunch. It is not uncommon for them to just want money, booze, transportation, weapons, and food. They may not believe the SF student team is capable of teaching them anything. © Hans Halberstadt

The SF student team leader discusses operations with the G chief. The students are immersed in the challenge of having to earn the respect of these resistance fighters but never compromising their own security, morals, values, or violating the military code of conduct. The Gs, on the other hand, do not respect the soldiers' values. The team must find ways, develop incentives, and influence the resistance fighters as to the merit of conducting operations their way. To the casual observer, this may seem like a game. It is not. This is serious business for any man hoping to someday wear a Green Beret. © Hans Halberstadt

The resistance fighters have now trained with the SF students and are preparing for one of their first confidence-building missions. The Special Forces team will accompany different elements of the resistance fighters into the mission. On this operation they launch a raid against a small enemy outpost. Each subsequent operation will be more challenging until the Gs are ready for the big one. The objective is to throw out the oppressive and tyrannical government. © Hans Halberstadt

Many of the role players in the Robin Sage unconventional warfare training exercise are Special Forces soldiers who have recently returned from combat assignments having worked with guerrilla resistance fighters. They are able to incorporate many personal lessons learned from this experience. © Hans Halberstadt

BMNT

Before morning nautical twilight is the time shortly before dawn when just enough light has developed to conduct military operations in the remaining shadows of night and yet see well enough without night-vision systems.

A student comments, "From this point on, it seemed like every hour we had some new critical decision to make. It got so that in nearly everything we did we had to ask ourselves, what's wrong with this picture?"

He continues: "The Gs tried to make us go places that would have almost certainly risked the entire team. They ridiculed our rules of engagement and even executed a prisoner right in front of us. Then they handed me the gun to shoot the next prisoner. When I refused, the G chief said, 'Okay then let's give the gun to the prisoner and see if he has the courage to shoot you?' After a couple of days of problem after problem and lack of sleep, we had to guard against over-evaluating everything. The Gs' ability to create an endless stream of complex decision-making scenarios was wearing us down. I think we eventually forgot that these guys were role players and just thought they were nuts!"

Another student tells this story: "While in isolation, our ODA asked for and received an agent from Pineland to brief us on the current intelligence, terrain, weather, etc. We thought we were very clever when we sent him back with much of our commo equipment and MREs [meals ready to eat] to cache for us in Pineland. This, of course, greatly reduced the amount of weight we would have carry.

"When we finally linked up with the Gs in Pineland, to our shock we learned that they had sold the radios, batteries, and MREs on the black market. Now, before we could launch our primary mission, we had to plan a raid on the black market to steal back these vital supplies and equipment. Fortunately, the Gs and their auxiliary decided to help out when they learned that much of the food was meant for them. We executed a 'direct-action' operation and retrieved the goods."

A recent Q course graduate and now an ODA detachment commander, who just returned from Afghanistan, talks about his experiences in Robin Sage: "Building and maintaining rapport with the Gs is the most critical task. The initial meeting with the G chief can make or break your experience for the rest of the scenario. Now is *not* the time to voice your food aversions, unless you have a serious religious or allergic reaction. Eat what is put in front of you—with vigor, if you can. Remember, that's probably a lot of food for them and considered a Pineland ethnic delicacy. You may want to offer to share with the G chief and his staff;

maybe they haven't eaten all day so they can offer you this 'snack.' The scenarios are endless, and you must always be thinking about what can go wrong next.

"Talk about yourself. Avoid being aloof. Be communicative. The G chief can be your best friend or worst enemy. Try to make him a friend. Avoid the standard, abrupt, direct communication that is popular with the military. Remember to concentrate on the G chief's likes and dislikes, his family, where he's from, and what he is going to do when it's all over. Too many of my peers only wanted to do the military operation and get out of Pineland as soon as possible. The more you believe and assimilate into the scenario, the easier it will be. Play the part. I really enjoyed Robin Sage (as you can tell)."

TRAINING THE GS

The ODA team sergeant comments, "We thought that we were never going to get these Gs to a stage where we could begin training them. In some ways they were training us. They were street smart and savvy, and we learned more than one lesson from them. Toward the end of the first week of the operation we were finally reviewing weapons and tactics and building an effective fighting force. We led the Gs on a series of combat missions of increasing difficulty. The G forces developed confidence in their abilities to engage the enemy. They learned how to conduct strikes on bridges, dams, and enemy outposts. The Gs were introduced to helicopter operational concepts. They were getting better by the day.

"Some of the Gs," the team commander adds, "were not in very good shape and we found that we had to constantly buy them transportation with local currency [Pineland DON], which resembled Monopoly money. The weapons sergeants had the toughest task of training the Gs in small unit tactics, and their operations orders were held to the same exacting standard as our own. No simplifying process was allowed. I did the best I could in 'training' the G chief in strategies, tactics, and mission planning. I managed to learn more from him instead of the other way around. The engineer and communications sergeants assisted the weapons guy as best they could, but our medic was busy treating the Gs and their myriad ailments. Fortunately, he had brought plenty of medical supplies and even used most of our own personal supplies to keep them going.

"There was at least one mission of some kind every day: a meeting with a local intelligence source that required a link-up, a message drop or pickup (sometimes by aircraft), a supply drop or cache recovery, reconnaissance, an ambush, or a raid. All required intense planning and execution. There was never a dull moment in the G base.

"Accountability of the Gs seemed to be our biggest challenge. They would wander off (to the 'secret' G base for food, water, or showers) and not tell anyone. They would fall asleep during movement and we would have to go back and find them. We actually had one G who headed into the woods to take a piss and got lost; we were up all night searching for him. We had to come 'out of role,' turn on all our lights, and call to him as we searched the surrounding area for him."

On this student ODA, the communications sergeant is also playing the role of the team's intelligence expert. He weighs into the commentary: "They were slowly coming around to respecting some Geneva Convention accords. But all was not well. On one combat mission, the Gs began a ritual of eating selected body parts of the slain enemy. Our team learned that the Gs' religion requires them to do this to prevent having to re-fight this enemy in the afterlife. It was very important to them that our ODA join them in this sacred ritual. Our team leader was asked by the G chief to carve out a body part of one of the dead enemy soldiers. The offer from the chief is considered an honor. How does a team leader respond? If you don't eat, you will seriously offend the men you have been

Women who work for the resistance fighters as "auxiliaries" brief the student ODA on enemy soldiers and equipment at the target area. Since almost no one can be completely trusted, the SF students are constantly searching for methods to determine the validity of information they receive. This could be a trap or it could be the key to victory. If their suspicions are obvious they risk losing support from these vital assets. Only a highly skilled Special Forces team will be able to figure this out. The clues are there if you think, listen, watch, and question with intelligence, cunning, and maturity. © Hans Halberstadt

working so hard to help. If you do carve and eat, you are in clear violation of the laws of land warfare. The least of your concerns are what it tastes like." (This part of the role playing is also based on real-world experiences of Special Forces teams.)

The entire ODA was grappling with the war-crimes problem. The weapons sergeant adds this: "Our Gs' Geneva Convention violation was the shooting of a prisoner during a raid. It was important that the ODA remember that the Gs are not signers of the Geneva Convention; however, if they want the U.S.' continued assistance and supplies, they must be held to that standard. Becoming indignant and threatening to report it to your chain of command is inappropriate, at best. Discuss the violation with the G chief and quietly report it in your next commo shot. Let the FOB decide whether to exfil you early or not."

As Robin Sage continues, students begin to unconsciously assimilate into the make-believe Pineland scenario. "You actually start feeling like you are in some hostile country," he says. He recalls being stunned back to reality when he noticed an American flag flying above the church that he was hiding in.

The Gs are ready for a major attack against the OPFOR. Your team meets with the area commander (the area command is the Special Forces B team). They too infiltrated into the country. The G force acquits itself well in the attack. Simultaneous attacks by G forces take place throughout Pineland. The oppressive government is defeated, but your team's problems are not over yet.

A guerrilla resistance fighter crawls low toward the enemy position during a raid. He is carrying a machine pistol, and his partner to the rear has a shotgun. Very often when Special Forces operates with resistance fighters in foreign countries they find that the Gs have a hodge-podge of weapons. © Hans Halberstadt

A Special Forces soldier in Afghanistan joins his resistance fighters in a cup of tea. When you compare this setting to the Unconventional Warfare training phase at the Q course, you can readily see the actual application in combat. Many Special Forces soldiers will later remark at how similar the training was to the cultural environment they found themselves in after graduation. The Special Warfare Center at Fort Bragg lives by the Army's motto, "You have to train like you fight."

IT AIN'T OVER 'TIL IT'S OVER

A student relates: "We congratulated the Gs on their victory, and they congratulated us. There were lots of happy faces everywhere until we asked the Gs to turn in their weapons. They refused!" Rogue bands of some not-so-happy Gs began to roam Pineland, taking whatever they wanted from the citizens. Their Special Forces teams had to find a way to stop this quickly. The Gs have become accustomed to power at the point of a gun. Your team has another complexity to resolve before this mission ends.

Finally, the Gs return to their farms, factories, and shops. They have turned in their weapons and are recognized as heroes throughout Pineland.

PHASE V
LANGUAGE SCHOOL

Depending on which Special Forces group you have been assigned to, Phase V will immerse you in language training appropriate to the part of the world in which you can expect to operate. For most students, Phase V will be somewhere between four and six months. However, following Phase V and VI, some students will be sent for further language training to the Defense Language Institute in Monterey, California. Chinese Mandarin or Arabic often require more than a year of schooling. Most students find the language training phase a great relief from the physical stresses they have endured in the previous four phases. It's a good time to relax and let your body heal before entering Phase VI. The principal instructors for each language are native speakers. Group study, language labs, and classroom instruction are the daily routine.

Four-month language courses taught at Fort Bragg:
French, Spanish, Portuguese

Six-month language courses taught at Fort Bragg:
Arabic, Czech, Russian, Korean, Persian, Polish
Serbo Croat, Thai, Tagalog

Your ODA returns to the original FOB facility and enters another brief isolation phase. The team reviews all the strengths and weaknesses of the mission, gathers all significant intelligence it collected. From experience, the teams offer insight on potential problems and players in the future of the Pineland government. You brief the FOB commander and his staff. And now comes the greatest wait: the SNCO cadre will identify those who passed and those who must recycle or leave the program. This is an agonizing wait.

Many factors—peer evaluations, "pink slips" (No Go), and "blue slips" (Go)—are taken into consideration to determine whether or not a student will continue or be recycled or dropped from the program. During the wait, a pall of silence falls on the Phase IV students. Everyone searches his soul and reviews his mistakes. The mood is a humble and somber one. They have all made mistakes. Some students struggle in vain to analyze the level of significance the mistakes have in the bigger scheme of things. Most will give up this futile analysis. It doesn't much matter now. What will be, will be. Many students have already purchased and painstakingly shaped their berets. But somehow one nagging question looms, "Will I be wearing a green beret tomorrow?"

After the completion of Robin Sage, many ODAs spend two or three days doing civic action projects to help the civilian role-players and contractors who support the program. They clean farms, do yard work, and mend fences. This helps maintain the good relationship between Special Forces and the local population. These locals get paid very little for their participation and do this only because they want to support the training and their country.

YOU'RE INVITED TO DINNER

You are one of the fortunate students who will be invited to the traditional regimental graduation dinner. You have been assigned to a Special Forces group. You are going to graduate from Phase IV and may now wear the coveted green beret. On your beret, you will wear your group flash, and you will also receive your group coin. The group flash is part of the uniform; the coin is part of a long-honored tradition.

You will have to wait for the final symbol of excellence, the Special Forces shoulder tab (sometimes called the "Long Tab"). The tab is only awarded after all SFQC phases are completed, but today your emotions are running high and you hardly know how to react. This moment has been a long time coming. A wide range of feelings overwhelm you. You know now that you really will finish the rest of your training. On this night you are joining an elite fraternity of best soldiers in the world. You have made it—almost.

SPECIAL FORCES GROUP COINS

Each SF group has developed an engraved coin that makes a symbolic or written statement that reflects that group's commitment to the country and the SF mission. In peacetime environments, an SF soldier must never be without his coin. Any SF soldier can opt to randomly challenge another SF soldier. He does so by slamming his coin on the table (often the bar). If the challenged soldier is not currently in possession of his coin to slam down in kind, he will have to buy everyone a drink. On the other hand, if the soldier being challenged does in fact slam down his coin, the challenger must buy the house a drink. It can be a costly mistake to forget your coin on any given evening.

MILES TO GO BEFORE I REST

The symbols of your Special Forces qualification are on loan to you. You may wear your Beret and Flash through the two phases remaining. The Army has a high degree of confidence that most of you who have reached this point will in fact successfully complete Phases V (language) and VI (Survival, Escape, Resistance, Evasion). If you fail V or VI, you will have to remove these symbols of extraordinary achievement and return to a regular Army duty assignment. On this day, there is not a soul present who can imagine such an outcome.

SEVEN SPECIAL FORCES GROUPS

(Five Active and Two National Guard)

1st Group, 3rd Group, 5th Group, 7th Group, 10th Group, 19th Group, 20th Group

The colors on each Special Forces group flash represent a slice of history unique to the legacy of that group. The current seven group flashes are (clockwise) 1st, 3rd, 5th, 7th, 10th, 19th, and 20th. The flash in the center is that of the 1st Special Warefare Center (the School House).

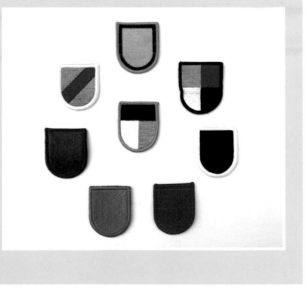

SEVEN

This prisoner is in severe solitary confinement. Days without light can begin to play tricks on the mind. Prisoners must begin to search for ways to win small victories. They must put something "over" on their captors. This is the path to regaining self-confidence and viewing captivity as just another challenge and not a defeat. It has been said that they must think of themselves as prisoners *at* war, not prisoners *of* war. © G. Schumacher

Phase VI: Survival, Escape, Resistance, Evasion (SERE)

OLD AND GRAY

They are old. Some are overweight. Some have beards or long hair, or no hair. You are in your final phase of SFQC. You are, of course, quite proud to have reached this point. These "old guys" are introduced as your subject matter experts (SME). Some students think to themselves that this has got to be some kind of gratuitous joke intended to pay homage to the "burned out." One student thinks to himself, "Okay, so let's get this part over with so that we can get on to real training."

Over the course of the next several days you will get to know the backgrounds of the SMEs. Some have nicknames like "Pops" or "Lizard" or "Crispy Critter." Little by little the personal stories of the SMEs come out. As you have already imagined, the SMEs were at one time some of the toughest men alive. They fought in places and survived in jungles that most of the students couldn't even pronounce. What most students don't realize is that, in many ways, these SMEs still retain more skill in their thumbnails than the SF students have learned in total.

A Special Forces NCO from the 3rd Special Forces Group works with local resistance fighters to develop their hand-to-hand combat skills. As with all Special Forces training, the SERE course martial arts training is not only about personal self-defense or quick-kill techniques, it is also about learning how to conduct martial arts training for foreign fighters.

THIS COULD HAPPEN TO YOU

The first four or five days is classroom training on survival techniques, escape and evasion planning, and, of course, more map reading. There is an element of storytelling during this first week as students listen to, analyze, and question the factual accounts of men who attempted to resist and survive in the hands of the enemy. You get a first-hand glimpse into the real dangers that you might face after graduation, which is only weeks away. In the words of one student, "I had wondered what more I could possibly learn in this last phase of SFQC. To my surprise, by the end of the third day I learned how much I didn't know."

Common to nearly all experienced SF soldiers is a quest for knowledge. It is not uncommon for these men to humbly comment on how much more they need to learn. When one considers that these are the best-trained soldiers in the world, that's quite a statement! A common denominator among all Special Forces men is that they seem to know what they don't know and they constantly strive to fill that knowledge gap.

FULL-FORCE HAND-TO-HAND COMBAT

"The hand-to-hand fighting we are going to teach you is not intended to inflict discomfort on your opponent. It is *not* intended to cripple your opponent. It is not intended to injure your opponent. What we teach you in this phase of your training is intended to *kill* your opponent in the quickest manner and with the least amount of expended energy.

"Never bring a knife to a gunfight," the instructor bellows. "What is your best defense against a physical attack?" The students offer a number of answers. "Wrong," says the cadre. "The best defense is not to *have* to fight. Here at the SERE course we say you need to *swoop*. In other words, run! Never fight if you don't have to. If someone is shooting at you, what do you do?" he asks. "Swoop," the chorus of students responds. "You got it!" answers the instructor.

The cadre continues, "Do not confuse your previous martial arts training with *our* training, known as LINEs (linear, infighting neuro-overide engagement). We will teach you how to counter and how to execute fatal blows.

When you fall, you will instinctively tuck and roll and return to your feet in the appropriate fighting posture. Throughout the rest of this phase you will fight your opponent with full force! You will not hold back. You will not fake a blow. You will not be timid. You will execute this training with the same intensity as if your fellow student were in fact the enemy! Students who are the opponent must counter your attack and execute full-force countermeasures on you. You are going to get bruised up, but if you pay attention to the instructors, you will walk away from each encounter. The only soldiers who get injured in this training are the ones who are not paying attention to the instruction."

The SNCO cadre goes on to explain, "LINE system training is a close-combat fighting technique that takes place in the grappling stages of hand-to-hand. Do not confuse it with self-defense. It is about killing the enemy in the quickest possible manner, under any conditions, night or day, regardless of whether you are the attacker or the one being attacked. Every move in LINE training is executed with two principles in mind. First, it must be medically supported that the technique can achieve the desired result on your opponent. Second, it must be technically feasible for you to execute the move without massive amounts of skill. LINE systems focus on 'learned muscle memory' that can be easily executed without having to consciously walk through the techniques." This is a good reason not to creep up on your Special Forces buddy in a dark alley.

SF students must train under the same conditions that they will experience in an actual situation. The Army's age-old phrase for this is, "Train like you fight!"

While the SERE course subscribes to the LINES form of martial arts training, each Special Forces group has the flexibility to explore other hand-to-hand combat training programs. The 1st Special Forces Group at Fort Lewis, Washington, has trained with Kelly Worden's International Spirit concepts. Worden is seen here teaching Special Forces soldiers how to disarm and overtake an opponent who is holding him at bay. The principles that Worden teaches concentrate on natural responses that don't require extensive memorization or repetition of unnatural moves. Worden calls it *Natural Reaction Defensive Tactics*.

The closer the combat environment can be replicated, the more effective the training experience. Another SF cadre addresses the group, "Gentlemen, you are well rested today, so it is a bad time to learn hand-to-hand combat. When the hour calls upon you that you should find yourself in a hand-to-hand situation, you are likely to be exhausted. So we will train in hand-to-hand when you are in full combat gear, tired, dirty, and hungry. If I determine that you are not sufficiently worn down prior to beginning the training, we will spend some time taking care of that issue first."

YOU'RE A DUCK, YOU'RE AN ALLIGATOR, YOU'RE A HIPPO, YOU'RE A SNAKE

As each of these commands is barked out by the cadre, students must mimic the behavior of the animal. The commands come down in torrents. This, as it turns out, is a technique used to sufficiently wear down students for a hand-to-hand class. Hand-to-hand training will be integrated into nearly every activity over the next four weeks. "Slap, grab, pull, kill" sequences of responding to an attacker are inculcated in every student. Slap the arm, grab the elbow, pull the attacker past you, execute the killing move with agility and strength. Counter, disable, and kill are the primary steps of an effective combatant. These moves must become instinctive.

GONE TO THE DOGS

Toward the end of week one, SERE students are introduced to the dogs: Attack dogs and tracking dogs are brought to the class. Many students take turns experiencing the methods used by attack dogs. That is, they suit up in protective gear and experience an actual attack. Subsequent review and analysis provide students with concepts for overcoming a dog attack. One student describes it this way, "You feel like you are the prey in some Wild Kingdom movie. The dog's level of intimidation can be very frightening!" The exposure to a dog attack helps students overcome their fear and develop reflex actions that will subdue the animal.

Students may also study tracking dogs. Bloodhounds are one of the breeds that are commonly employed in scent tracking. Students learn techniques that are useful in confusing and disorienting the dogs. They develop an appreciation for the incredible skills these animals have. This will be an important consideration in their escape-and-evasion planning.

During the first week of SERE training, dog handlers, like the soldier in this photo, will familiarize students with techniques of both attack and tracking dogs. Some students will experience being attacked by a highly trained canine. Instructors will focus on techniques to overcome a dog attack. They will also discuss differences between search and cadaver dogs.

THE DINNER MENU

What's for dinner? Rabbits, chickens, and goats garnished with sides of bark, roots, and leaves with a sprinkling of insects. Toward the end of week one, the students are trucked out to the field. They have a small quantity of water and no food. You and the SMEs (Graybeards) are going to survive under the same conditions. It will soon become very apparent to you that the Graybeards are light years ahead of you in conquering the elements. Almost effortlessly, and in just a few minutes, they have a fire going, a shelter built, and are drinking coffee while cooking food on the grill. Some students are frustrated and can't even get their fire going. Not surprisingly, students begin to creep up on the Graybeards to see just what they have done. Fortunately, after this brief lesson in humility is over, the Graybeards are eager to share their field craft skills with the students.

For this first part of survival training, the meat portion of dinner will be *provided . . .* alive. Thereafter, no more free meals. You will kill, gut, clean, prepare, and examine the animals for disease. You learn how to determine if a plant is edible or poisonous without the aid of a book or picture. From here on, if you want meat, you will have to catch it.

Since you are not the first Special Forces student to be hunting in these woods, the local animal life has gotten pretty darn good at avoiding hungry students. Necessity will play a role in helping you quickly learn how to snare wild animals. Some starving students have been known to outrun a rabbit. After a few days of hunger, it should come as no surprise that food that was distasteful on day one is a gourmet meal on day five.

You will begin to learn about "human" trackers and "sign cutters." What you are learning will be vital to

This animal trap, called the "simple dead fall," can be used to drop a large boulder to kill prey or, as pictured here, it is being used to capture prey. The pointed end of the stick that is parallel to the ground is baited, and the sticks are notched at joining points.
© G. Schumacher

SERE students are taught how to catch, clean, and consume both fur and fowl. Chickens are a readily available commodity for training purposes. The skills learned in plucking, gutting, and cleaning a chicken are applicable to other bird species. © G. Schumacher

A Special Forces soldier demonstrates how to humanely and quickly kill a chicken. The chicken is calmed and hypnotized by drawing a line directly in front of its eyes. A stick is then placed over the neck and holding onto to the breast, the head is separated from the body. (If you hold on to the legs you will have a pair of legs in your hand and one very upset chicken.) Every part of the chicken is put to use. The blood is captured in a metal can or bowl and can be used to lure other animals, cooked as nutritious blood cake, or drunk to prevent hydration. The bones are used to enhance weapons and construct fish hooks. The feathers are used to develop a warm pillow or garment, and the meat is ravenously consumed. © G. Schumacher

SERE students learn the most effective methods for capturing and killing fur-bearing animals. Held upside down, as in this photo, the rabbit is struck at the bend in the neck with the knife edge of the hand. The neck is broken and the animal instantly dies. There is no suffering. © *G. Schumacher*

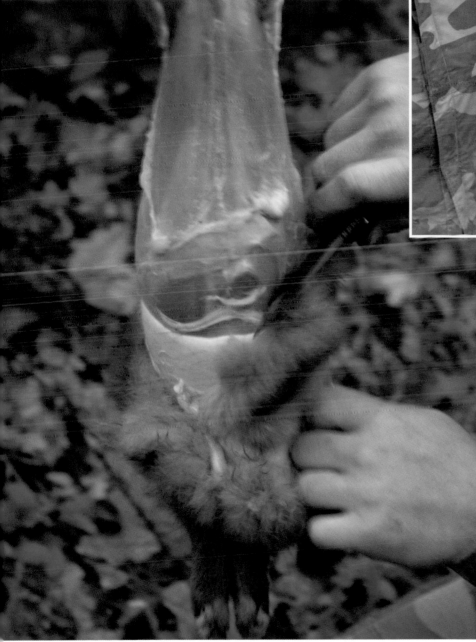

The dead animal is suspended from a branch. Students practice the proper methods of skinning and gutting the animal with care taken to not contaminate the meat with urine or fecal matter. After gutting and cleaning, SF students are taught how to examine the meat to ensure it is not diseased or infected. And finally, cooking methods are reviewed and the prey is consumed. © *G. Schumacher*

125

successfully planning for and evading capture during the resistance training lab (RTL). RTL is the final week of SERE. Sign cutters are at the highest level of tracking skills category and often work in pairs. They can identify their target's track even after a site has been badly contaminated by other searchers. They will find your track, determine length of stride, direction, and speed. Often they will leapfrog forward to validate the first indications. It is very difficult to escape a good sign cutter, but knowing how they operate and whether the enemy has those capabilities can be of value. Considerations of how and when to establish movement patterns and break patterns are vital to your survival in a hostile environment when the enemy has sophisticated capabilities.

SELF-CARE AND IMPROVISED MEDICINE

Occasionally, your digestive tract won't respond well to some of the exotic cuisine that you are consuming. No problem. Mix up some homemade anti-diarrhea treatment from wood ash. Got a burn that needs attention? Whip together a paste of tannic acid from leaves and bark and get some soothing relief. You will learn how to draw out infection and many more basic survival skills. Your classroom training from the first week now turns into practical applications throughout week two.

DIVIDE AND CONQUER

Around the start of week three you will return to the classroom to study methods an enemy might use to break down the morale of their American captives. To quote SFC Ken Sterns, a former instructor at the SERE course, "There is no one that cannot be broken. What we attempt to do is show them methods that may be used against them in a captive environment. Special Forces personnel armed with this knowledge can often thwart the enemy's intentions. The Special Forces prisoner is taught how to maintain some semblance of personal identity, morale, and a positive association with fellow prisoners. If the enemy can turn prisoners against one another, they will quickly exploit this advantage."

SERE students are expected to craft weapons from whatever they can scrounge while on the run from the enemy forces in hot pursuit. These makeshift weapons were produced inside of an hour and show what can be done in a hurry with a little imagination. As with shelters, crude, makeshift weapons will be improved upon daily as time permits. © G. Schumacher

Challenged to invent hunting and fishing tools to meet basic food survival requirements, students make these simple fish lures from available materials. The fish hooks can be crafted from nails, twigs, bone fragments, collar insignias, tin, and tiny pieces of cloth. Fish line can be made from tarpaulin or canvas by raveling the threads and tying groups of short lengths together. © G. Schumacher

SFC Sterns continues, "Often the techniques the enemy uses are so subtle that prisoners are not even aware they are being used. Most students, on the other hand, are certain, that in a training environment this pitting of one student against another could never happen. Quite to the contrary, the SERE staff expertly manipulates class after class. The SF cadre are very efficient at generating divisiveness among the students and causing the students to work for their captors' objectives. In the end, when this becomes obvious, the students have been humbled, but they have also been educated.

"Successful resistance comes in small packages," says SFC Sterns. "Prisoners must find ways to survive one minute, one hour, one day at a time. They must incorporate a series of small victories wherever the opportunity presents itself. It is through these small victories that a prisoner can retain some sense of control over his environment."

Students are introduced to different styles of interrogation and discuss the pros and cons of resistance methods. The methods of interrogation and methods of resisting are classified information and cannot be revealed on the pages of this book.

INCONSPICUOUS

As the third week winds down, the "low-profile" aspect of Green Berets begins to take root. Special Forces students quickly learn that the less visible they are as individuals, the less attention they draw, thus the greater likelihood of their continued survival. They learn how to melt into civilian populations when they are abroad.

They learn not to be the "Ugly American." There is a noticeable absence of boisterous "chest pounders" in the Special Forces community. This culture of becoming the "quiet professional" will be so ingrained in their psyches that you will rarely hear of their exploits. That's the way SF prefers it.

By way of example, in the 1970s, in preparation for a planned hostage-rescue mission, former Special Forces personnel were inserted into the Iranian city of Tehran.

This soldier is attempting an escape. The students' paradox is that if they fail in an escape attempt they will be severely punished. In actual captivity they would probably be executed. Yet if they pass up clear opportunities to escape this will hold badly for them in the course evaluations. © G. Schumacher

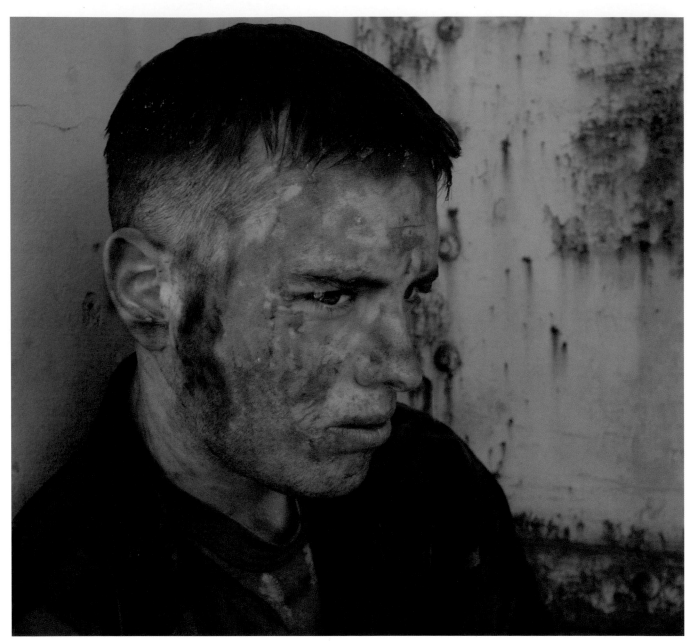

As escape becomes more and more problematic or seemingly futile, prisoners go through a period of self-incrimination. They begin to feel as if they have failed. They feel as if they let their comrades, their family, and their country down. They internalize that their predicament is somehow their fault. If they are to resist a complete mental breakdown they must learn to deal with and overcome these negative emotions. © G. Schumacher

They were disguised in various civilian capacities. These men were able to move among the population without drawing undue attention. They gathered intelligence that was essential to the final operational plan. In the end, thousands of Iranian soldiers were searching everywhere for them. The men successfully executed escape and evasion plans that resulted in their safe return home.

RESISTANCE TRAINING LAB (RTL)

This is the graduation exercise. An SF cadre explains the scenario, "You are deep behind enemy lines. You must move toward friendly lines and will receive missions at various points along the way. Hundreds of soldiers from the 82nd Airborne Division are searching for you. They are the enemy. If you are caught, they will take you to a prison. This enemy does not abide by the Geneva Convention rules regarding treatment of prisoners of war. If captured, you will be treated as a criminal." We overhear a student make the comment, "No way, no how, not gonna happen." He is clearly referring to not getting captured. A few days later we notice a student prisoner wearing the same student number. We can't see his face because he has a bag over his head and he is handcuffed. It's a safe bet that this is the same "no way, no how student."

Students move by night and sleep by day. They have to build shelters in locations least likely to be discovered by the enemy. They cannot use roads or trails. They must eat off the land and take care to camouflage their cooking fire. Students have to conceal their tracks and execute all of the evasion techniques they have been taught. The terrain is unforgiving. They will be wet, cold, tired, bruised, thirsty, and hungry. One SERE graduate says, "In the beginning I would avoid likely locations of snakes. By the end, I was picking up every rock and log looking for a decent meal."

Many students will be caught, some sooner rather than later. How *soon* is the primary difference. Some students who ultimately make it all the way to link up with friendly forces have forgotten the correct link-up authentication procedure. The consequences are that the student is suspected of being an enemy spy by the friendly forces and is either killed in the attempt to cross lines or is taken prisoner.

As you near the end of your mission, you might have to travel by car through local towns. At various points, armed enemy guards halt your vehicle. Your ability to maintain a false identity is critical to your survival. Finally, you are mere yards from freedom with one last checkpoint to get through. A simple mistake now would result in capture and make it all for naught. Will you make it?

You are captured. Students have learned that the best time to successfully escape is as soon as possible after capture. As a prisoner is transported to other facilities, the level of expertise of the guarding forces will increase at each step, thus making it increasingly difficult to make a break. Also, when first captured, you might be close to friendly forces and the enemy is moving fast to avoid pursuit. During this period they guard themselves as well as you. The deeper you are moved into enemy territory the more attention they will be able to focus on you. Some students

attempt an escape. Some fail. Those who fail face severe punishment at the hands of their captors; however, if a student has a clear opportunity to escape but doesn't see it, this will be incorporated into his evaluation.

Welcome to the prison. You are disoriented, hungry, tired, and apprehensive. You are confident that you will not fall victim to the enemy's methods. You resist being exploited with all your will. They want you to sign some papers to denounce America. They also want you to cooperate in a propaganda video. You are slapped around but continue to resist. "Okay," says your interrogator, who has one of the smallest prisoners brought forward. They begin dunking him. They begin slapping him. Each time you refuse to cooperate they get rougher with him; the punishment intensifies. The student taking the punishment for you is in bad shape. Still more prisoners are punished. You helplessly watch as they suffer because of you. What do you do?

FINDING WAYS TO RESIST: A POW STORY

Colonel Stephen Leopold, a Special Forces officer and personal friend of the author, was captured by the enemy when he was a young lieutenant. He was knocked out by an explosion and woke up in enemy hands. Leopold spent more than six years as a prisoner of war in Vietnam. During that time he was transferred from prison camp to prison camp.

For many of the early years he was locked in bamboo cages under a triple-canopy jungle in Cambodia. Hungry, isolated, and often abused, he and his fellow prisoners made a pact. They could either laugh or cry. They could either feel sorry for themselves or they could have fun. They chose to have fun.

When the guards made prisoners teach them English, they concentrated on sexual terms, which made the guards extremely uncomfortable and uneasy. Many of guards began to avoid the prisoners' language training program.

(Note: Only trained and specified cadres are authorized to slap. They have practiced the proper method over and over on one another. They have had done to themselves tenfold whatever they might do to a student. This is carefully monitored.) Sophisticated techniques of pitting groups of students against one another are used. Some students don't see it. Some see it but are helpless to stop it. Some think they are beating the enemy's strategy, but in fact they are playing right into it. Some break down completely. This experience becomes the most unforgettable training you will ever know. And so it should be.

Now comes the day of the graduation. Those who failed are no longer there. Like casualties on the battlefield, you cannot long dwell on their misfortune. You have made it. Today you are going to graduate from SFQC. You experience part disbelief. Surely, you think to yourself, there must be some minefield to cross between now and the graduation ceremony. You have emerged from a life-changing experience, never to be the same man again. What you have become is more important than what you've done to get here. In one sense it was a lifetime ago that you entered Phase I, and yet in another it was only yesterday.

Throughout the rest of your life you will encounter people who will boast, "They wanted me to be a Green Beret." And that may be true. After all, the Army would like nothing more than to have lots of Special Forces soldiers. Still others will falsely claim to have been Green Berets. Such a façade is completely transparent to the men who have actually completed the Q course. Those who are can clearly discern those who aren't.

Completion of SERE training marks the formal end of the Q course and the end of your long journey to become a U.S. Army Green Beret. You will wear the "long tab" on your left shoulder. You will know that you are now part of the "quiet professionals:" the finest warriors the world has ever produced, *sine pari* (without equal).

Captured students are covered and tied up during transport to the POW camp. This will make it more difficult for them to know where they are in the event one should escape. It also promotes mental confusion and disorientation. Opportunities to escape are generally more likely early in the captivity process. © G. Schumacher

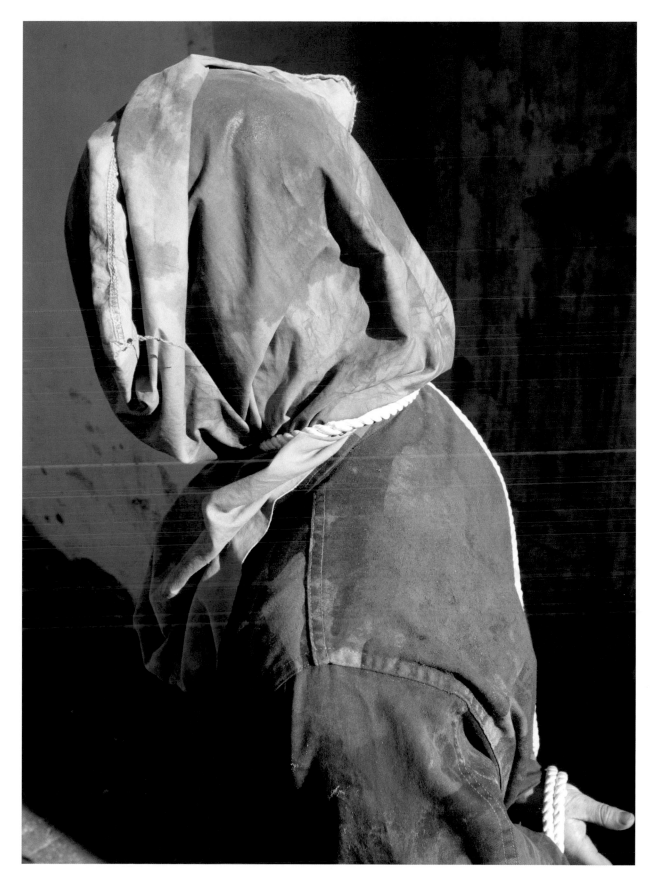

EIGHT

Students emerge from a tactical night dive on the ready. During the course they will learn how to use both open-circuit and closed-circuit rebreathers. Closed-circuit systems eliminate air bubbles that would otherwise ascend to the surface. In still waters the bubbles might be detected and could compromise the mission. *© Hans Halberstadt*

Follow-On Training

Each Special Forces group trains for missions in primary and secondary areas of the world. Within those large geographical areas, for example Southeast Asia, the SF battalions, companies, and teams require additional training in languages and ODA-specific missions. There are literally hundreds of courses that Special Forces students might attend. Some of them are very exotic. Some of them are classified "Secret" and cannot be revealed here. There are several critical training courses that many SF soldiers will pass through in their careers. They are Arctic, Jungle, Desert, Combat Diver, Sniper, and Military Free Fall. Those SF soldiers who don't attend all of these courses will have been exposed to training by those who have. This is what SF calls "train the trainer."

It is not uncommon for SF soldiers to periodically change teams or even SF groups during their careers. Consequently, as they join each new SF group, soldiers have to get oriented and trained in their new group's environment and missions. All of the Q course graduates will get a whole lot more training before they hang up their spurs. Here is a typical story of a recent Q course graduate:

"I was excited to finally be joining up with my unit. I had checked in with the battalion and then the company headquarters. I got a bunch of 'welcome aboards' from the sergeant major and the guys at the company level. The company commander sent for the detachment commander, and he brought me in to meet the team. I was really looking forward to my first real SF mission. I had barely begun to unpack when

An instructor descends into the 50-foot dive tank at the U.S Army's Combat Diver Qualification School. Students must perform a 50-foot free ascent. The dive tank is also used to teach "buddy breathing" and other underwater techniques.
© Hans Halberstadt

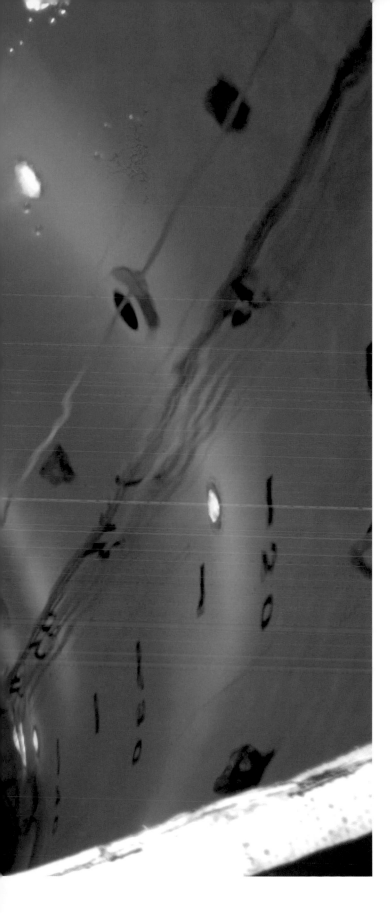

the team sergeant said, 'Don't get too settled in; we need you to head off for the Special Forces Underwater Combat Divers Course.' I didn't know whether to laugh or cry. It had been nearly three years of training for me to reach this point, and the first thing I'm told is that I'm not trained enough. My ODA, as it turned out, was assigned SCUBA missions in our area of operations. I now realize it would not have mattered much which team I was assigned to. Every ODA in our company had some kind of mission that required further schooling. A couple of weeks later I was in Key West, Florida."

BY LAND, BY AIR, BY SEA

These three concepts of infiltration are what the three lightning bolts on the Special Forces patch represent. To meet that requirement you are one of many Special Forces Q course grads now on your way to the U.S. Army Combat Divers Qualification Course (CDQC) at the Trumbo Point Annex Naval Air Station in Key West. CDQC is one of several courses offered by the SF Underwater Operations School. For the next four and a half weeks you will study maritime operations and subsurface water infiltration techniques. Your training will include open-circuit SCUBA and closed-circuit rebreather operations. The underwater operations include underwater search-and-recovery and lock-in and lock-out submarine operations.

During the first week of the Combat Divers Qualification Course, students must demonstrate swim capabilities and underwater composure. Instructors will interfere with submerged students to remove fins and masks, disengage valves, and use other forms of harassment with the intent to observe how the students respond in an underwater environment under stress. © *specialtactics.com*

An instructor checks fittings and conducts a visual safety inspection on students prior to their first "sea" dive. The Combat Divers Course requires students to perform both day and night navigation dives of 500 to 2,000 meters. © Hans Halberstadt

A Special Forces student stands in formation receiving final instructions prior to a daylight navigation dive. Each Special Forces Group has specific requirements for ODAs capable of conducting underwater operations. Recent attendance at the Special Forces Underwater Operations School have increased dramatically and many Q course graduates will find themselves in this program shortly after they receive their Special Forces tab. © Hans Halberstadt

A student emerges from a daylight tactical dive. In addition to underwater gear, breathing systems, masks, fins, and so on, he is lugging his weapon, ammunition, and a rucksack. All of it soaked with water. As one student comments, "When I broke the surface and began movement to secure the beach, I felt as if the force of gravity had multiplied 10 times the normal level." © *Hans Halberstadt*

Special Forces students at CDQC are taught techniques for using submarines as infiltration and exfiltration platforms. Two of the methods to accomplish this are lock-in and lock-out and decks awash. Lock-in and lock-out are accomplished from a submerged submarine. Decks awash requires the sub to surface, which most submariners would prefer not to do in a combat zone. In the above photo, a Los Angeles class attack sub breaks the surface just off the coast of Crete, Greece.

Although small boat operations are taught throughout Special Forces training, CDQC has recently expanded its training to include advanced special operations small boat training. Kayaking is one of several new classes added to the course and has proven to be a very useful mode of clandestine transportation. © *Fred Pushies*

Early in this course you will go through the "ditching and donning" test. All of your gear, including tanks and weights, is 15 feet below the surface and you must remain underwater while putting all of this on beginning with only one breath of compressed air. You will also swim underwater for an hour while instructors harass you by removing your fins, mask, oxygen tanks, and so on. The objective is to test your underwater composure. If you fail either of these tests you are removed from the course. Underwater navigation is stressed throughout the course and you will complete day and night navigation dives ranging from 500 to 2,000 meters. During the training, students will swim distances in excess of 30 kilometers.

Open circuit training includes navigation and search dives, submarine operations, a 130-foot-deep dive, and 50-foot free-swimming ascent. Closed circuit training consists of team dives and establishing a beach-landing site. CDQC focuses extensively on rebreather operations. Recently added to CDQC are small boat operations, casting and recovery, maritime air operations, and nautical navigation and charts.

A Special Forces combat diver, on a post-training operation, describes a "decks awash" mission: "It was about 2:30 in the morning and an extremely black night. The sea was quiet and still like a dead pond. We had loaded into our Zodiac about an hour earlier and headed out to sea for our pickup by submarine. In the black stillness, suddenly the sub broke the surface like a monster of the sea. It was surreal. I felt like our little inflatable was a gnat on an elephant's ass."

MILITARY FREE-FALL PARACHUTE COURSE (MFFPC)

Up to this point all of the jumps you have made have been what is known as "static line." Static line means your parachute is attached to a cable inside the aircraft and the chute pulls open as you fall away from the plane. Your jumps might have been done with parachutes that are somewhat more steerable than the parachutes that conventional units use, but up until now that was the only major difference. There are actually four methods of parachuting into your target area: Static line, HALO, HAHO, LALO.

A group of free fall students sit in the hangar waiting for their aircraft. This will be a "Hollywood" jump (no equipment or weapon). In these early phases, students will practice altitude awareness, tracking, mid-air assembly, canopy control, and proper alignment on approach, base, and final landing patterns. © Hans Halberstadt

Most people are familiar with High Altitude, Low Opening (HALO) jumping because in some ways it is similar to skydiving. An SF student refers to skydiving as "Hollywood" jumping because skydivers, for the most part, jump in daylight, without equipment, over a huge and well-marked drop zone. The SF students must jump with a whole bunch of equipment and weapons, and often from altitudes requiring cold-weather suits and oxygen masks. And, oh yes, at night with no ground markers. HALO is a common method of infiltration, and quite a few SF soldiers will be sent to this training.

While at the Military Free Fall course, SF soldiers will also train and practice High Altitude, High Opening (HAHO) jumps. This technique of opening your chute at very high altitudes can be an exhilarating experience with lots of "hang time" (the amount of time you float beneath your canopy). This is, of course, provided that your team has properly calculated where the jet stream is before jumping. HAHO jumpers can track for well over 30 miles before reaching the ground. The military's modified ram-air squares can provide a glide speed of 25 miles per hour. HAHO techniques provide excellent cover (low radar signature) for an ODA attempting to infiltrate into an enemy country without having to fly directly over the target area.

The first week of MFFPC is conducted at Fort Bragg. The week starts with classroom instruction on exit techniques, basic body positions, stabilizing, tracking, and using the horizon to acquire situational awareness. You will study the air foil characteristics of "squares." Squares are rectangular parachutes with a series of parallel vents passing from front to rear. You will rehearse

These 1st Special Forces Group soldiers conduct a HALO "tailgate jump" (exiting off the back ramp of an aircraft) from a CH-46E Sea Knight Marine Corps helicopter. Notice the lead jumper's body flipping vertically, appearing to almost tumble. The jumper will maintain the proper body position, and in a few seconds his body will stabilize parallel to the ground and face down. Their acquired discipline through training keeps their mind and body responding with the proper techniques throughout the descent.

This jumper's rucksack is considerably smaller than the loads normally carried on a static-line jump. For this reason, there are times when a low-altitude static-line insertion is the only method that makes sense. The rucksack is secured by a spider harness. Improved spider harnesses have recently been introduced. On the other hand, prepositioned equipment or low-flying jets may jettison a pod to resupply a team that has made a free-fall insertion. © Hans Halberstadt

A free-fall student on his "final" prepares to land. He has lowered his rucksack and is turning into the wind. This action of turning can be seen on close examination because the jumper's right arm is up and his left is pulling down. The MC5 ram-air "square" parachute he is using is primarily used for free-fall jumps, but it can be rigged under special circumstances for a static-line exit. Just a few feet above the ground the jumper will pull down hard on both toggles to stall the parachute's momentum for a safe landing. *© Hans Halberstadt*

Two Military Free Fall students and their instructor gather up their chutes after an on-target landing. Students are required to land within 25 meters of the group leader. Evidently these three came in on roughly the same spot. During the course, each student is paired with another student approximately the same size. This helps ensure a similar rate of descent. Each pair has a group leader/instructor with them at all times.
© Hans Halberstadt

over and over again procedures for checking your altimeter at specific intervals. You need to learn to check the altimeter without wreaking havoc on your stability in the air. You will learn the meaning of free-fall parachuting terms like approach, base, and final, and precisely when to "stall" the chute on landing. As the week comes to a close, you will get your turn in the wind tunnel.

The wind tunnel produces air currents of 150 miles per hour and simulates the conditions of actually falling through the sky. On your introduction to the wind tunnel you will first watch as cadre float like birds, seemingly effortlessly, changing positions and directions at will. Then it's your turn. Suddenly, it doesn't seem so effortless. You struggle to maintain body position. You tumble and slide with the currents. It will take some practice and concentration for you to master the physical attitudes required to emulate the cadre. You learn to develop the correct body arch, recover from a tumble, check your altimeter, and simulate pulling your rip cord. Some students get pretty banged up in the tunnel, but better a few bruises here than suffering the consequences of the same mistake in the sky.

After you have mastered the vertical wind tunnel, you will go out to Yuma desert in southern California, where you will study exiting different types of airframes and begin to practice high-altitude free falls with full equipment. During the course you will make about 28 free-fall jumps. In your second week, you will exit at 17,500 feet wearing oxygen gear and carrying combat equipment. You will learn how to perform a mass exit and how to group with other jumpers in the sky in both day and night jumps. Now you are going higher each day and will execute a minimum of two HAHO jumps requiring oxygen and a cold weather suit. One of those jumps must be with full combat gear. As one student laughingly recalls, "The golden rule is that if you find yourself passing other jumpers in the air, don't think that you are winning the race!"

During the first week of Military Free Fall School, students go through wind tunnel training. Once in the tunnel, a giant fan blows the air at around 150 miles per hour. Students will practice their body position and simulate checking altitude and stabilizing. Mistakes can earn you a few bruises. Notice the padded walls in the background.
© Hans Halberstadt

Above: The V22 Osprey is the newest addition to aircraft used to deploy Special Forces teams. This aircraft has vertical take-off and landing capabilities that can plant an ODA anywhere in the world without regard to airfields or large dirt runways. It is far faster than helicopters and can carry a much larger load. As seen in this photo, the Osprey is deploying heat-seeking missile defense systems using advanced survivability technology.

Left: The U.S. Army Special Operations jump team, appropriately named "The Black Daggers," exit from a chopper on a demonstration jump and begin the creation of a star formation on their way down.

Upon graduation from MFF students are awarded their free-fall wings. The dagger, again, represents the stealth methods employed by Special Operations units. It is laid over a tab that symbolizes the skill identifier tab worn by Special Operations soldiers. The wings represent flight and the parachute is a seven-cell square, the MT-1X, which was the first chute to be adopted by all U.S. military Special Ops units. © Hans Halberstadt

A group of free-fall students head out for a night jump. During the course the students will make as many as 28 jumps and quite possibly more, depending on weather conditions. On HALO (High Altitude, Low Opening) students generally jump from between 10,000 and 17,000 feet and deploy their chutes around 3,500 feet. © Hans Halberstadt

SNIPER SCHOOL

Many Special Forces soldiers, 11-Bravos in particular, attend the Army's Sniper School at Fort Benning, Georgia, which is officially called the Special Operations Target Interdiction Course (SOTIC). The sniper's primary weapon system is the M24 7.62-millimeter bolt-action rifle with adjustable butt stock and a 10-power scope. It has an 800-meter effective range.

"Most soldiers think that good marksmanship is what this course is all about," comments an instructor. "Have no doubt that marksmanship is important, but most of you seriously underestimate the significance of other critical sniper skills. Becoming an Army sniper is about self-discipline, self-reliance, self-control. It is about tracking, stalking, deception, ranging, and surviving. It is about operating independently, with patience and cunning. And finally, it is about shooting straight and shooting true—on the *first* shot every time."

He goes on, "Any amateur can occasionally hit his target with one shot; it is the professional sniper who hits every target every time he fires—with but one, single, solo, round downrange. Your standard infantryman can miss a few shots here and there. He has men on his left and right to pick up the slack. The sniper can *never* afford to miss. The enemy will respond boldly to a 'missed' shot, but they will be far more cautious when one among them has experienced a direct hit. And that's one less person firing back at you." The instructor closes with this comment, "On the battlefield, the U.S. Army sniper is the 'Phantom of the Opera.'"

A U.S. Army Sniper stalks behind this mask of broken patterns and blending colors. The irregular shape of the manufactured material covering his face has been scientifically designed and is extremely effective, but snipers can produce equal or even superior cover with natural grasses and twigs.
© Hans Halberstadt

A pair of snipers blend into the dry grass. The barrel of their M500 .50-caliber RAI sniper rifle is clearly visible for the photograph but would normally be completely camouflaged also. Snipers must be good enough to accurately take out a target nestled among many other people at distances out to 2,000 meters.
© Hans Halberstadt

SF Snipers use this laser target designator, which is a "passive" infrared viewer. At night this device will provide an image of any object that emits heat, called a heat signature. Unlike "active" infrared devices, the enemy cannot detect the location of the user because it does not emit a visible or infrared beam.
© Hans Halberstadt

The M24, bolt-action, 7.62mm sniper rifle seen here is mounted with an SU-87/PBS4 scope. The rifle has been around for quite some time and will likely remain a favorite for military snipers well into the future. It is a close cousin of the civilian Remington Model 700. Scopes, however, are constantly improving in both weight and capabilities, and upgrades are always just around the corner. © Hans Halberstadt

A sniper has a clear kill shot through his 10x scope mounted atop an M24 rifle. Any shooter has a lucky shot on occasion, but a sniper cannot depend on luck. He has no force protection, and when he fires, a miss could mean his life. Few combat soldiers have the time to contemplate their actions in taking an enemy's life, but conversely the sniper can think and anticipate what he is about to do. This requires a strong psychological base and a deep courage of conviction. © Hans Halberstadt

Sniper School is no cakewalk, even for Special Forces graduates. It is a very exacting course and has no tolerance for kinda, sorta, maybe performance. Either you are completely camouflaged and melt into the environment or you are a wannabe who hasn't paid sufficient attention to detail. Wannabes don't make it. Either you can remain motionless for hours and stalk silently, or you are a bull in a china shop and

A student sniper stalks his target. Getting into position within an effective range may take him hours. The sniper must gauge the natural effects and timing of wind on the surrounding vegetation and use it to cover his movement. If an instructor spots his movement or can identify his position he has failed that segment of training. He must have a first-round hit.

Snipers work in pairs and cover one another. They are often sent into areas where the only comrade within miles of their position is their fellow sniper. The two must anticipate each other's action and almost telepathically communicate their moves. The sniper must have extraordinary self-discipline and patience. The senior member of the team is the spotter who will identify the target and determine distance.

need to roam somewhere else. Either you hit the target at 600 meters on the first round, or you seek some other skill, like writing regulations. This is a no-nonsense course that has some of the highest entry prerequisites in the Army.

ARCTIC, SUBARCTIC, AND MOUNTAINEERING

Special Forces soldiers assigned to SF groups that have mountain or cold-climate area missions will often be sent for additional training to Army's Northern Warfare Training Center in Fairbanks, Alaska. From there they proceed to the Black Rapids Training site at Delta Junction. This area is called the "bowl" because it is in the central interior of Alaska, surrounded by mountains. The bowl boasts some of the coldest temperatures on the planet. The bowl can be colder than even the North Slope of Alaska, which is above the Arctic Circle. This is because there are no ocean breezes to moderate the temperatures. Winter temperatures often range between -50 and -70 degrees. That's not counting windchill.

Before you can begin running around the frozen tundra, you need to learn a few hard facts about basic survival in this extreme environment. One SF soldier explains, "First you can't run around sucking in cold air or you will freeze your lungs. You have to extend your oversized parka hood way out in front of you with a small opening to see and breathe. This is called the *warming chamber*.

Ice fog is generated from human activities at Fort Wainwright near Fairbanks, Alaska. This is January and the temperature is 60 degrees Fahrenheit. The barometric pressure is extremely high. There is no wind. The sun has just risen at 11 a.m. The ice fog will continue to get worse as the vehicles and people emit moisture vapor throughout the short day and well into the evening. In a few hours, visibility may be measured on a yardstick. A single aircraft taking off will sometimes create so much ice fog that the airfield must be closed for 24 to 48 hours. © G. Schumacher

"On many winter days the air can be totally still, dry, and perfect for ice fog. Ice fog is created by the expelling of any warm, moist air from a car, a plane, or your breath. If a plane takes off, you won't be able to see 2 feet through the thick blanket of ice fog that will remain the entire day. If you are on a patrol, everywhere your patrol moves will boast a thin trail of ice fog for the entire day, the same as a plane's vapor trail at high altitudes. When you camp out for the night, there will be little vapor clouds above the site where you pitched your tent for the entire next day. The air in your vehicle tires will crystallize and flatten the tires; you'll be driving on a square wheel. When you toss your hot coffee into the air, it turns into brown ice balls before it hits the ground."

Soldiers dig in a hasty fighting position. When working in a cold-weather climate, care has to be taken to allow perspiration to evaporate and not soak into the interior clothing. Fluids must be consumed regularly to prevent dehydration. This is a fact that many people fail to consider in cold climates. © Fred Pushies

"If you don't have the ice fog, you have the wind. When it is 50 below zero and the wind is gusting through the mountains at 20 miles per hour, you can freeze the fluid in your eye socket by just facing into the wind. I can tell you a lot of chilling stories about the challenges confronting the Bear [cold weather]," he concludes.

Almost as an afterthought he adds, "Speaking of bears, the black bears are in hibernation, so you don't need to worry about them, and besides, when they come out of hibernation, they have to get their digestive tracts working with fruits and berries for the first couple of weeks. It will be a week or two before they start hunting you. As for the polar bears, you had better not shoot one unless you can prove that it was already dining on some part of your anatomy."

Students quickly learn that every move they make in this climate has to be preceded by a survival analysis. Reaching for a piece of metal, drinking fluids, breathing air, or walking a hundred yards requires thought and planning. You can take nothing for granted. Your cold-weather training will include frostbite prevention, signs of hypothermia, building fires in deep snow, constructing shelters, water procurement and treatment, snow cave construction, and when and where to build a fire pit.

An SF soldier relates one of his Alaska cold-weather stories: "It was the dead of winter and we had set up camp out near the Bering Strait. It should have been a warning to us when we saw that the houses in the local villages were all built on stilts. Nevertheless, we pitched a tent and got a little careless in laying out the ground cloth. We got a little heat generated, ate, and crashed for the night. I guess we were on frozen marshland. During the night the ice thawed just enough to let out a layer of mosquito eggs. We woke up to trillions of starving, biting mosquitoes in our tent. We were running across the ice in our BVDs slapping ourselves. What a sight that must have been! Who'da thunk it in January?"

Learning to conduct military operations under these conditions is a basic requirement of Special Forces groups with this area orientation. You will navigate, cross-country ski, rappel, mountain climb, study ice bridges, test cold-weather first aid, learn how to hunt, fish, and prepare and consume fluids in an arctic environment. In the mountaineering training you learn how to use ropes and rope-work management, ice-axe training, rigging for glacier travel, basic rescue techniques, terrain and snow pack analysis, and route selection.

A Special Forces communications sergeant emplaces his satcom radio. The temperature in these areas has been known to get so cold that coax cable on radio sets can simply crack in half like a piece of glass. Fluids can coagulate and make refueling and other operations very challenging. © Fred Pushies

Arctic warfare is taught at the Army's Northern Warfare Training Center in Alaska. SF students will study and experience fighting and surviving in extreme snow and cold weather conditions. The effects of arctic weather on both equipment and personnel are unique. Nothing can be taken for granted in this unforgiving environment. © Fred Pushies

JUNGLE WARFARE TRAINING

Some trainees are assigned to groups whose areas require advanced jungle training. Both the 1st Special Forces Group, which covers Southeast Asia (Philippines, Malaysia, Burma, and so on) and the 7th Special Forces Group, which employs ODAs to Central and South America, have extensive requirements for expertise in tropical and sub-tropical environments. The U.S. Army's Jungle Operations Training Center (JOTC) is at Fort Sherman, Panama. Over the years, many Special Forces teams have actually rotated through as instructors at the school. Depending on which SF group you are assigned to, you may well find yourself spending time both as a student and as an instructor in this wet water wonderland.

"The jungle can be your friend or your enemy," comments an instructor. "If you respect it and its inhabitants, it will provide you with an abundance of food, water, shelter, and medicine. On the other hand, for the ignorant and unprepared, it will be certain death. Tens of thousands of people worldwide continue to die from malaria. Others perish from dysentery, yellow fever, dengue fever, and dozens of other 'alphabet soup' diseases. The fighter who can make the jungle his friend can turn it into the demise of his enemies."

The JOTC has every type of jungle feature rolled into one chunk of land: mountains, swamps, blue water, brown water, elephant grass, and single and double-canopy jungle. The density of some jungles can turn daylight into night. The sun never shines into this thick morass of dense, wet, bug-infested vegetation. As one student describes it, "It's the land version of the bottom of the sea, complete with sea monsters that have no eyes."

This is the setting where you execute land navigation, undertake water-borne operations, and conduct reconnaissance and patrolling operations. You develop hygiene skills to prevent your skin from contracting "jungle rot" (a very potent cousin of athlete's foot and jock itch). You learn how to remove bloodsuckers and how to treat cuts and injuries. In tracking classes you learn what signs indicate that someone has moved through a part of the jungle before you. Most important, you learn the sounds and the smells of the jungle. As one SF soldier put it, "Long before your eyes tell you what trouble is ahead, your ears and nose will be sounding the alarm. Learn to listen to the jungle."

DESERT SURVIVAL TRAINING

Given the large number of military operations in the Middle East, it is no wonder that many Special Forces soldiers attend desert survival training. Special Forces A teams have been frequently infiltrated deep into remote desert areas to hunt for isolated mobile missile sites or fulfill reconnaissance needs. Regardless of which SF group you are assigned to, the requirement for further desert training is going to be a must. Many of the SF

An ODA moves across the California desert on a training mission. Special Forces teams frequently participate in desert training at the Army's National Training Center, Fort Irwin, California. Fort Irwin is adjacent to Death Valley and about 30 miles from the town of Barstow. This is an excellent location to prepare for deployments to the Persian Gulf region. © *Fred Pushies*

groups have developed their own desert training programs, and several contract this training to civilian institutions that are frequently operated by, you guessed it, former Special Forces soldiers. This is what you can expect: As with all training programs, your desert operations training begins in the classroom. You must learn how to conquer the three challenges of desert survival: heat, water, and cold. You learn the indicators of heat exhaustion and its progressive cousin, heat stroke. You study and practice methods for procuring and preparing water. This includes finding sinkholes and springs, harnessing dew, draining fluids from vegetation, and building water stills. Finally, you have to prepare for frigid desert nights and know the signs of hypothermia.

The desert flash floods and desert windstorms have been known to kill many unsuspecting campers. A cloudburst miles away at higher elevations can roll a wall of water down on top of thirsty men without warning. You will learn the terrain features and weather indicators that could place your team in just such a life-threatening situation.

Some say that everything in the desert either bites, stings, or burns. In that vein you will study desert wildlife such as scorpions, spiders, snakes, and reptiles. You'll find out that a certain desert tortoise carries its entire year's supply of water within its body. If you pick it up, the water discharges and the tortoise will die. As one survival course student says, "It doesn't take a rocket scientist to figure out that you collect the water and eat the tortoise." Well you better eat every last bit of it, including the shell, because this particular breed of wildlife is on the endangered species list, so you will have to justify near-death circumstances if you happen to resort to this expedient during a training exercise.

One SFer relates, "We were at the Army's National Training Center, at Fort Irwin, about 50 miles outside of Barstow, California. This is just spitting distance from Death Valley in the Mojave Desert. You get a real feel for how horrible these desert conditions are when coyotes stalk you at night. The damn things are so scrawny that you feel sorry for them. They are four-legged skeletons. They are starving to death. You are going to have to be

Rock-climbing skills are not just nice to have, they are essential for many SF missions. This Special Forces soldier in Afghanistan is working his way up a sheer vertical wall. His teammates are following. Friction climbing, face and crack climbing techniques, and multi-pitch climbing are learned and practiced. Anchors, knots, belays, rope management, rappelling, and lower techniques are just some of the skills SF students will master in their mountain-climbing training.

Desert survival training includes learning to cope with severe desert sandstorms. A sandstorm in this photo is about to overtake a 3rd SF Group ODA operating in Afghanistan. Like a tropical cloudburst, a sandstorm can emerge at almost any time. To those caught unprotected and exposed, a sandstorm can be fatal. These storms have been known to bury vehicles and shut down helicopters in flight.

A 7th Special Forces Group soldier, high over South America, peers out the aircraft window just prior to a free-fall jump. The large gauge on his wrist is his personal altimeter that he will check many times during descent. Special Forces soldiers sometimes exit the aircraft wearing oxygen at altitudes over 25,000 feet, and they deploy their chutes almost immediately. They will then track laterally for dozens of miles before touching down. This technique is known as HAHO (High Altitude, High Opening).

smarter than Wile E. Coyote if you expect to survive. There are a lot of myths about water stills and getting water from cacti. The energy expended in making water stills usually more than offsets the net gain of one-half cup a day, and many of those cacti have toxic substances. If you have no alternatives, I guess that's what you've gotta do, but those are some pretty desperate measures with some potentially ugly consequences."

Your desert training might take place in the deserts of California or the sands of Kuwait. One way or another, you'll get your parched lips. We're reminded by a recent graduate of desert training that, "It's those damn baby rattlers that you gotta watch out for. The big ones conserve some of their poison for future prey. They just want you to go away. It's those little suckers that pour *all* their venom into you. They just don't have any self-discipline."

LIVE ENVIRONMENT TRAINING (LET)

Following the SERE course, many Special Forces soldiers are sent to Live Environment Training. This training places you in an urban environment in which you encounter a myriad of good guys and bad guys. Many of the people you run into are very unsavory. You are on a specific mission that cannot be compromised. Some the characters you interact with are role players in the exercise. Others are actually the local people, police, and officials who may or may not know who you are or that you are in Special Operations training. You won't know who's who. This training will prepare you to operate within urban communities, to conduct reconnaissance, develop intelligence networks, and execute other Special Operations missions.

The Meadows Vacation and the Richmond Training Phase are classified training exercises. If you remember, early in this book I told you that some former SF soldiers had infiltrated Iran as businessmen during the planned Iranian hostage rescue mission. The leader of this group was Dick Meadows. Good Luck!

Index

To Be a U.S. Marine
ISBN 0-7603-1788-7

To Be an FBI Special Agent
ISBN 0-7603-2118-3

To Be a U.S. Air Force Pilot
ISBN 0-7603-1791-7

To Be a U.S. Army Ranger
ISBN 0-7603-1314-8

To Be a U.S. Navy SEAL
ISBN 0-7603-1404-7

Hunting al Qaeda
ISBN 0-7603-2252-X

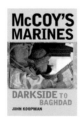

McCoy's Marines
ISBN 0-7603-2088-8

Delta
ISBN 0-7603-2110-8

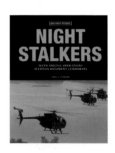

Night Stalkers
ISBN 0-7603-2141-8